CHARLES LATHRAM

My Walk With Him

Copyright © 2024 by Charles Lathram

All rights reserved. No part of this publication may be reproduced, stored or transmitted in any form or by any means, electronic, mechanical, photocopying, recording, scanning, or otherwise without written permission from the publisher. It is illegal to copy this book, post it to a website, or distribute it by any other means without permission.

Charles Lathram asserts the moral right to be identified as the author of this work.

Charles Lathram has no responsibility for the persistence or accuracy of URLs for external or third-party Internet Websites referred to in this publication and does not guarantee that any content on such Websites is, or will remain, accurate or appropriate.

First edition

This book was professionally typeset on Reedsy.
Find out more at reedsy.com

Contents

Prologue — 1

I Dedication

1. Then Along Came My Lord — 5
2. Turn Thorns into Triumph — 12
3. On Borrowed Time — 19
4. Why Burdens Can Be Blessings — 31
5. When God Asks for It Back — 37
6. When I Am Doing So Well, I Forget to Do Good — 43
7. Please, I'm Sorry and Thank You — 49
8. Less Like Me and More Like You — 55
9. Why "No" May Be the Best Answer — 61
10. The Power of Forgiveness — 67
11. On a Different Road — 73
12. Living on Borrowed Grace — 79
13. He Was Holding My Hand — 85
14. I am Weary, but With You I Can Prevail — 91
15. Mercy is His Love, Undeserved — 97
16. Whatever Happens, Rejoice in the Lord — 103
17. What Do I Have That He Has Not Given — 109
18. Please Don't Judge as I Deserve — 115
19. He Died is My Why — 121

20	When All Fades Away, He Remains	127
21	For Love and Grace	133
22	I Am But Clay in the Potter's Hands	139
23	But for the Grace of God, Go I	145
24	As for Me, I Will Serve the Lord	151
25	To Whom Shall We Go	157
26	Not My Will, But Your Will Be Done	163
27	He Is More Than Enough	169
28	You Are My Firm Foundation	175
29	My Cross Cannot Compare	181
30	Lead Me Home	187

Afterword   193

Prologue

~~~~~~

Dear Reader,

Welcome to a journey of faith, introspection, and divine connection. This book is a labor of love, born from my experiences of seeking solace, guidance, and strength through prayer. Each chapter is a heartfelt prayer crafted into a poem that reflects the myriad ways we encounter God's presence in our lives.

In moments of joy and sorrow, triumph and trial, I often turn to prayer to communicate with God. Through these intimate conversations, I have come closer to Him, finding comfort in His promises and strength in His unwavering love.

This collection of prayers as poems is designed to be a companion in your spiritual journey. Each chapter is not just a prayer but a reflection of the human (at least my own) experience intertwined with hope in Him. Following each poem, you will find a relevant Bible verse, offering scriptural grounding and deeper insight into the themes explored. Reflections

My Walk With Him

and guided prayers are included to help you meditate on the messages and apply them to your life. By no means am I an expert in matters of Faith, but I have become an expert in begging Him for help, strength, and comfort, and He has never failed me.

My hope is that this book will inspire you, uplift you, and bring you closer to God's heart. May it serve as a reminder that in every season, whether in times of abundance or in need, God is always near, holding our hand and guiding our steps.

With warmth and compassion,

Charlie

Dedication

*To Mom,
Thank you for who you are and who you inspired us
to be. I love you!*

One

Then Along Came My Lord

Welcome, I am so happy that you chose to walk along this journey with me. I hope that you will find inspiration, hope and in the end, feel a bit closer to Him. Let's begin.

Then Along Came My Lord

In the dawn of life, when dreams were new,
   Through the morning mist, the skies so blue,
   I walked with hope, my heart so light,
   Then along came my Lord, my guiding light.

Through the ups and downs, the highs and lows,
   In the darkest nights, when the cold wind blows,
   He held my hand, He heard my plea,
   Then along came my Lord, to comfort me.

My Walk With Him

In the times of joy, when laughter rang,
   In the moments of sorrow, when my heart sang,
   He was my strength, my shield, my armor, my sword,
   Then along came my Lord, my faithful Lord.

When victories crowned my weary brow,
   And failures tried to bring me down,
   He lifted me, He made me strong,
   Then along came my Lord, all along.

All I have is from His grace,
   All I am through His embrace,
   Let me never forget, in every accord,
   Then along came my Lord, my eternal reward.

Reflection

In this chapter, we walk with the Lord through the various stages of life. From the dawn of our journey, He serves as our guiding light, illuminating our path and filling our hearts with hope. As we traverse through life's ups and downs, His comforting presence reassures us, holding our hands and listening to our pleas. In moments of joy and sorrow, He stands as our strength, our shield, and our sword, faithfully supporting us.

When we face victories and failures, His strength lifts us up, renewing our spirit and giving us the courage to continue. Finally, we acknowledge that all we have comes from His grace, and all we are is shaped by His loving embrace. Let us never forget that in every moment, He is our eternal reward, guiding us with His unwavering love.

This chapter reminds us that walking with Him means experiencing His presence in every aspect of our lives. It encourages us to trust in His guidance, find comfort in His presence, draw strength from His support, and be grateful for His grace. Let us begin this journey of faith, knowing that He is with us every step of the way.

When We Look, What We Find

Guiding Light in New Beginnings
"In the dawn of life, when dreams were new,
Through the morning mist, the skies so blue,
I walked with hope, my heart so light,
Then along came my Lord, my guiding light."

Bible Verse
"The Lord is my light and my salvation—whom shall, I fear? The Lord is the stronghold of my life—of whom shall I be afraid?" (Psalm 27:1)

Inspirational Insight:
Context: Psalm 27 is all about King David's rock-solid faith, even when things got tough. He knew God was his protector and source of courage. This verse is like a warm hug, reminding us that God is our guiding light, chasing away fear and filling us with strength. Just like the poem says, God's presence brings hope and light into our lives, making our hearts feel light and free. With Him by our side, we can face anything without fear.

My Walk With Him

Comfort in Times of Trouble
"Through the ups and downs, the highs and lows,
In the darkest nights, when the cold wind blows,
He held my hand, He heard my plea,
Then along came my Lord, to comfort me."

Bible Verse:
"Even though I walk through the darkest valley, I will fear no evil, for you are with me; your rod and your staff, they comfort me." (Psalm 23:4)

Inspirational Insight:
Context: Psalm 23 paints a lovely picture of God as our shepherd, always guiding and protecting us. This verse is like a cozy blanket on a cold night, reassuring us that we're never alone. God's comforting presence is always with us, offering peace and solace. Just like in the poem, He holds our hand through life's ups and downs, listening to our pleas and providing comfort, just like a shepherd care for his flock.

Strength in Joy and Sorrow
"In the times of joy, when laughter rang,
In the moments of sorrow, when my heart sang,
He was my strength, my shield, my sword,
Then along came my Lord, my faithful Lord."

Bible Verse:
"The Lord is my strength and my defense; he has become my salvation." (Psalm 118:14)

Inspirational Insight:

Then Along Came My Lord

Context: Psalm 118 is a joyful celebration of God's never-ending love and deliverance.
This verse is like a pat on the back, reminding us that God is our rock-solid source of
strength and protection. Whether we're laughing with joy or singing through sorrow,
God stands by us as our strength and defense. The poem reflects this beautifully,
showing how His faithful presence empowers us to face life's challenges with
confidence and grace.

Renewed Strength in Triumphs and Failures
"When victories crowned my weary brow,
And failures tried to bring me down,
He lifted me, He made me strong,
Then along came my Lord, all along."

Bible Verse:
"But those who hope in the Lord will renew their strength. They will soar on wings like
eagles; they will run and not grow weary, they will walk and not be faint." (Isaiah
40:31)

Inspirational Insight:
Context: Isaiah 40 is a message of hope and encouragement to the Israelites,
promising God's restoration and strength. This verse is like a breath of fresh air,
reminding us that hope in the Lord renews our strength. It

ties back to the poem by
   showing how God lifts us up and makes us strong, whether we're celebrating victories
   or facing failures. With His strength, we can rise above our struggles and soar to new
   heights, just like eagles.

Grace and Eternal Reward
   "All I have is from His grace,
   All I am through His embrace,
   Let me never forget, in every accord,
   Then along came my Lord, my eternal reward."

Bible Verse:
   "For it is by grace you have been saved, through faith—and this is not from yourselves, it is the gift of God." (Ephesians 2:8)

Inspirational Insight:
   Context: The Apostle Paul wrote to the Ephesians to highlight the amazing power of
   God's grace and the gift of salvation. This verse is like a gentle reminder, capturing
   the essence of grace as a beautiful, unearned gift from God. It ties perfectly with the
   poem, emphasizing that everything we have and everything His loving embrace
   shapes us. It inspires us to live with gratitude, recognizing that our lives are a
   testament to His grace and eternal reward.

Then Along Came My Lord

Questions for Personal Reflection or Group Discussion

- How have you experienced God's guidance in your life?
- In what ways has God provided comfort during difficult times?
- How can you remind yourself of God's grace and eternal reward in your daily life?

Guided Prayer

- "Dear Lord, thank You for being my guiding light and my strength in times of need. Help me to always trust in Your presence and find comfort in Your embrace. Amen."

Two

Turn Thorns into Triumph

Hello again! In this chapter, we'll explore how God can transform our struggles into triumphs. We'll see how our thorns can become His triumphs through heartfelt poetry, meaningful scripture, and uplifting insights. Let's walk this path together and find hope and strength in His grace.

Turn My Thorns into Your Triumph

In the journey of my life, with trials and strife,
   Through the pain and the tears, the struggles of life,
   Let me see my burdens in a different light,
   Turn my thorns into Your triumph, make it right.

When the weight of the world feels too much to bear,
   And my heart is heavy with sorrow and care,
   Instead of asking for the pain to cease,

Turn Thorns into Triumph

Turn my thorns into Your triumph, bring me peace.

In moments of suffering, when hope seems lost,
   And I question the path, the journey, the cost,
   Let me find strength in the lessons they bring,
   Turn my thorns into Your triumph, let my heart sing.

For every struggle is a chance to grow,
   To show Your love, to let it flow,
   Through my trials, let Your glory shine,
   Turn my thorns into Your triumph, make it divine.

Help me to see beyond my own pain,
   To the lives I can touch, the love I can gain,
   In every hardship, let me find the way,
   To turn my thorns into Your triumph, every day.

Let my life be a testament to Your grace,
   In every challenge, let me find my place,
   To glorify You, to make others' lives bright,
   Turn my thorns into Your triumph, with Your light.

Reflection

In this chapter, we explore how God can turn our thorns into triumphs. From seeing our burdens in a new light to finding peace in heavy hearts, we learn that our struggles can lead to growth, strength, and divine triumphs. By touching others' lives and being a testament to His grace, we can transform our hardships into opportunities to glorify God.

My Walk With Him

This chapter encourages us to trust in God's purpose, find comfort in His presence, and draw strength from His grace. Let's continue this journey of faith, knowing that He can turn our thorns into His triumphs every day.

When We Look, What We Find

Seeing Burdens in a New Light
   "In the journey of my life, with trials and strife,
   Through the pain and the tears, the struggles of life,
   Let me see my burdens in a different light,
   Turn my thorns into Your triumph, make it right."

Bible Verse:
   "And we know that in all things God works for the good of those who love him, who have been called according to his purpose." (Romans 8:28)

Inspirational Insight:
   Context: Romans 8:28 is a powerful reminder that God can bring good out of any situation for those who love Him. This verse encourages us to see our burdens in a new light, knowing that God is working behind the scenes for our good. It ties back to the poem by reminding us that our struggles can be transformed into triumphs through His divine purpose.

Finding Peace in Heavy Hearts
   "When the weight of the world feels too much to bear,
   And my heart is heavy with sorrow and care,
   Instead of asking for the pain to cease,

Turn Thorns into Triumph

Turn my thorns into Your triumph, bring me peace."

Bible Verse:
"Come to me, all you who are weary and burdened, and I will give you rest." (Matthew 11:28)

Inspirational Insight:
Context: Matthew 11:28 is an invitation from Jesus to find rest and peace in Him. This verse is like a soothing balm, offering rest to our weary hearts. It aligns with the poem by showing that instead of seeking an end to our pain, we can find peace and triumph in God's comforting presence.

Strength in Suffering
"In moments of suffering, when hope seems lost,
And I question the path, the journey, the cost,
Let me find strength in the lessons they bring,
Turn my thorns into Your triumph, let my heart sing."

Bible Verse:
"Consider it pure joy, my brothers and sisters, whenever you face trials of many kinds, because you know that the testing of your faith produces perseverance." (James 1:2-3)

Inspirational Insight:

Context: James 1:2-3 encourages believers to see trials as opportunities for growth and perseverance. This verse invites us to find joy and strength in our suffering, knowing that it builds our character and faith. It ties back to the poem by highlighting that our trials can lead to triumphs, making our hearts sing with newfound strength.

Growth Through Struggles
"For every struggle is a chance to grow,
To show Your love, to let it flow,
Through my trials, let Your glory shine,
Turn my thorns into Your triumph, make it divine."

Bible Verse:
"But he said to me, 'My grace is sufficient for you, for my power is made perfect in weakness.' Therefore, I will boast all the more gladly about my weaknesses, so that Christ's power may rest on me." (2 Corinthians 12:9)

Inspirational Insight:
Context: 2 Corinthians 12:9 reveals how God's grace and power are magnified in our weaknesses. This verse reassures us that God's grace is enough, and His power shines through our struggles. It ties back to the poem by showing that our trials can become divine triumphs, displaying His glory and love.

Touching Lives and Gaining Love
"Help me to see beyond my own pain,
To the lives I can touch, the love I can gain,
In every hardship, let me find the way,
To turn my thorns into Your triumph, every day."

Bible Verse:
"Praise be to the God and Father of our Lord Jesus Christ, the Father of compassion and the God of all comfort, who comforts us in all our troubles, so that we can comfort those in any trouble with the comfort we ourselves receive from God."

Turn Thorns into Triumph

(2 Corinthians 1:3-4)

Inspirational Insight:
Context: 2 Corinthians 1:3-4 highlights how God comforts us so we can comfort others. This verse encourages us to look beyond our pain and use our experiences to touch others' lives. It ties back to the poem by showing that our hardships can become triumphs as we gain love and offer comfort to those around us.

A Testament to Grace
"Let my life be a testament to Your grace,
In every challenge, let me find my place,
To glorify You, to make others' lives bright,
Turn my thorns into Your triumph, with Your light."

Bible Verse:
"For it is by grace you have been saved, through faith—and this is not from yourselves, it is the gift of God." (Ephesians 2:8)

Inspirational Insight:
Context: Ephesians 2:8 emphasizes the transformative power of God's grace and the gift of salvation. This verse reminds us that our lives are a testament to God's grace. It ties back to the poem by highlighting that in every challenge, we can find our place to glorify God and make others' lives brighter through His light.

Questions for Personal Reflection or Group Discussion

My Walk With Him

- How have you seen God transform your struggles into triumphs?
- What lessons have you learned from your moments of suffering?
- How can you use your experiences to touch others' lives and offer comfort?

Guided Prayer

- "Dear Lord, thank You for turning my thorns into triumphs. Help me to see my struggles in a new light and find strength in Your grace. Guide me to use my experiences to comfort and touch others' lives. Amen."

Three

On Borrowed Time

Hey there! Welcome to another chapter of our journey of faith and discovery. In this chapter, we'll explore the concept of living on borrowed time and how recognizing this can bring us closer to God. Through poetry, scripture, and uplifting insights, we'll see how He gives us strength and purpose in every moment.

On Borrowed Time

In the story of my life, with twists and turns,
   Through sunny days and times that burn,
   I walk this road, both rough and fine,
   Knowing I live on borrowed time.

Through the highs of joy and lows of pain,
   In wins and losses, sunshine and rain,

My Walk With Him

He gives me strength, His love's the sign,
Knowing I live on borrowed time.

In the laughs we share and tears that fall,
   In moments big and moments small,
   He shows me grace, a gift so kind,
   Reminding me always, it's on borrowed time.

When things go right and shadows creep,
   In life's garden, where dreams sleep,
   He whispers softly, 'This life's mine,
   Live it fully, it's on borrowed time."

May I repay Him with acts of love,
   With a heart that reaches up above,
   In every step, in every climb,
   Remembering always, it's on borrowed time.

Reflection

In this chapter, we're reminded of the preciousness of our time on earth and the importance of living each moment with purpose and gratitude. Recognizing that our time is borrowed encourages us to value every day, find strength in God's love, embrace His grace, and live fully for His glory.

We are called to express our love for God through our actions, serving others and making a positive impact in the world. This chapter inspires us to live each day with a heart full of gratitude, knowing that every moment is a gift from God.

On Borrowed Time

When We Look, What We Find

Acknowledging Life's Temporary Nature

"In the story of my life, with twists and turns,
Through sunny days and times that burn,
I walk this road, both rough and fine,
Knowing all I have is on borrowed time."

Bible Verse:
"Teach us to number our days, that we may gain a heart of wisdom." (Psalm 90:12)

Inspirational Insight:
Context: Psalm 90 is a prayer of Moses, reflecting on the brevity of life and the importance of wisdom. This verse reminds us to value each day and live wisely, knowing our time on earth is limited. It ties back to the poem by emphasizing the temporary nature of life and the importance of making the most of every moment.

Finding Strength in God's Love

"Through the highs of joy and lows of pain,
In wins and losses, sunshine and rain,
He gives me strength, His love's the sign,
For all I have is on borrowed time."

Bible Verse:
"The Lord is my strength and my shield; my heart trusts in him, and he helps me." (Psalm 28:7)

Inspirational Insight:

Context: Psalm 28 expresses David's trust in God as his protector and source of strength. This verse reassures us that God is our strength and shield, helping us through life's ups and downs. It aligns with the poem by highlighting how His love and strength support us, even as we live on borrowed time.

Embracing Grace and Gratitude
"In the laughs we share and tears that fall,
In moments big and moments small,
He shows me grace, a gift so kind,
Reminding me always, it's on borrowed time."

Bible Verse:
"But he said to me, 'My grace is sufficient for you, for my power is made perfect in weakness.' Therefore, I will boast all the more gladly about my weaknesses, so that Christ's power may rest on me." (2 Corinthians 12:9)

Inspirational Insight:
Context: In 2 Corinthians, Paul speaks of the sufficiency of God's grace in all circumstances. This verse highlights the power of God's grace in our lives, especially in our weaknesses. It resonates with the poem by reminding us to embrace His grace with gratitude, recognizing that every moment is a precious gift.

Living Fully for God's Glory
"When things go right and shadows creep,
In life's garden, where dreams sleep,
He whispers softly, 'This life's mine,

On Borrowed Time

Live it fully, it's on borrowed time.'"

Bible Verse:
"So whether you eat or drink or whatever you do, do it all for the glory of God." (1 Corinthians 10:31)

Inspirational Insight:
Context: Paul encourages the Corinthians to live their lives in a way that honors God in all things. This verse calls us to live fully for God's glory, in everything we do. It ties back to the poem by encouraging us to live each moment purposefully, knowing our time is borrowed and meant to reflect His glory.

Acts of Love and Service
"May I repay Him with acts of love,
With a heart that reaches up above,
In every step, in every climb,
Remembering always, it's on borrowed time."

Bible Verse:
"Dear children, let us not love with words or speech but with actions and in truth." (1 John 3:18)

Inspirational Insight:
Context: John emphasizes the importance of showing love through actions, not just words. Hey there! Welcome to another chapter of our journey of faith and discovery. In this chapter, we'll explore the concept of living on borrowed time and how recognizing this can bring us closer to God. Through poetry, scripture, and uplifting insights, we'll see how He gives us strength and purpose in every moment.

My Walk With Him

On Borrowed Time

In the story of my life, with twists and turns,
    Through sunny days and times that burn,
    I walk this road, both rough and fine,
    Knowing I live on borrowed time.
    Through the highs of joy and lows of pain,
    In wins and losses, sunshine and rain,
    He gives me strength, His love's the sign,
    Knowing I live on borrowed time.
    In the laughs we share and tears that fall,
    In moments big and moments small,
    He shows me grace, a gift so kind,
    Reminding me always, it's on borrowed time.
    When things go right and shadows creep,
    In life's garden, where dreams sleep,
    He whispers softly, 'This life's mine,
    Live it fully, it's on borrowed time."
    May I repay Him with acts of love,
    With a heart that reaches up above,
    In every step, in every climb,
    Remembering always, it's on borrowed time.

Reflection

In this chapter, we're reminded of the preciousness of our time on earth and the importance of living each moment with

On Borrowed Time

purpose and gratitude. Recognizing that our time is borrowed encourages us to value every day, find strength in God's love, embrace His grace, and live fully for His glory.

We are called to express our love for God through our actions, serving others and making a positive impact in the world. This chapter inspires us to live each day with a heart full of gratitude, knowing that every moment is a gift from God.

When We Look, What We Find

Acknowledging Life's Temporary Nature
"In the story of my life, with twists and turns,
Through sunny days and times that burn,
I walk this road, both rough and fine,
Knowing all I have is on borrowed time."
Bible Verse:
"Teach us to number our days, that we may gain a heart of wisdom." (Psalm 90:12)
Inspirational Insight:
Context: Psalm 90 is a prayer of Moses, reflecting on the brevity of life and the importance of wisdom. This verse reminds us to value each day and live wisely, knowing our time on earth is limited. It ties back to the poem by emphasizing the temporary nature of life and the importance of making the most of every moment.

Finding Strength in God's Love
"Through the highs of joy and lows of pain,
In wins and losses, sunshine and rain,
He gives me strength, His love's the sign,
For all I have is on borrowed time."
Bible Verse:
"The Lord is my strength and my shield; my heart trusts in him, and he helps me." (Psalm 28:7)
Inspirational Insight:
Context: Psalm 28 expresses David's trust in God as his protector and source of strength.
This verse reassures us that God is our strength and shield, helping us through life's ups and downs. It aligns with the

poem by highlighting how His love and strength support us, even as we live on borrowed time.

Embracing Grace and Gratitude
"In the laughs we share and tears that fall,
In moments big and moments small,
He shows me grace, a gift so kind,
Reminding me always, it's on borrowed time."
Bible Verse:
"But he said to me, 'My grace is sufficient for you, for my power is made perfect in weakness.' Therefore, I will boast all the more gladly about my weaknesses, so that Christ's power may rest on me." (2 Corinthians 12:9)
Inspirational Insight:
Context: In 2 Corinthians, Paul speaks of the sufficiency of God's grace in all circumstances.
This verse highlights the power of God's grace in our lives, especially in our weaknesses. It resonates with the poem by reminding us to embrace His grace with gratitude, recognizing that every moment is a precious gift.

Living Fully for God's Glory
"When things go right and shadows creep,
In life's garden, where dreams sleep,
He whispers softly, 'This life's mine,
Live it fully, it's on borrowed time.'"
Bible Verse:
"So whether you eat or drink or whatever you do, do it all

for the glory of God." (1 Corinthians 10:31)

Inspirational Insight:

Context: Paul encourages the Corinthians to live their lives in a way that honors God in all things. This verse calls us to live fully for God's glory, in everything we do. It ties back to the poem by encouraging us to live each moment purposefully, knowing our time is borrowed and meant to reflect His glory.

Acts of Love and Service

"May I repay Him with acts of love,
With a heart that reaches up above,
In every step, in every climb,
Remembering always, it's on borrowed time."

Bible Verse:

"Dear children, let us not love with words or speech but with actions and in truth." (1 John 3:18)

Inspirational Insight:

Context: John emphasizes the importance of showing love through actions, not just words. This verse encourages us to express our love for God through our actions and service to others. It aligns with the poem by reminding us to use our borrowed time to perform acts of love and kindness, reflecting God's love in everything we do.

Questions for Personal Reflection or Group Discussion

- How does recognizing that our time is borrowed change

On Borrowed Time

your perspective on daily life?
- In what ways can you express your gratitude for God's grace in your actions?
- How can you live more fully for God's glory in your everyday activities?

Guided Prayer

"Dear Lord, thank You for the gift of life and the precious moments You grant us. Help me to live each day with purpose, gratitude, and love, reflecting Your glory in all that I do. Amehis verse encourages us to express our love for God through our actions and service to others. It aligns with the poem by reminding us to use our borrowed time to perform acts of love and kindness, reflecting God's love in everything we do.

My Walk With Him

Questions for Personal Reflection or Group Discussion

- How does recognizing that our time is borrowed change your perspective on daily life?
- In what ways can you express your gratitude for God's grace in your actions?
- How can you live more fully for God's glory in your everyday activities?

Guided Prayer

"Dear Lord, thank You for the gift of life and the precious moments You grant us. Help me to live each day with purpose, gratitude, and love, reflecting Your glory in all that I do. Ame

Four

Why Burdens Can Be Blessings

Hey there! Welcome to another chapter of our journey of faith and discovery. In this chapter, we'll explore the idea that our burdens can be blessings in disguise. Through poetry, scripture, and uplifting insights, we'll see how God uses our struggles to teach us, strengthen us, and reveal His love.

Why Burdens Can Be Blessings

In the journey of my life, with its ups and downs,
    Through the smiles and the tears, the laughs and the frowns,
    I seek to understand, with a heart that's confessing,
    Why burdens can be blessings, Your gifts in disguise, impressing.

When trials come my way, and the road gets tough,
    And I feel overwhelmed, like I've had enough,

My Walk With Him

    Help me see the strength, in each challenge I'm addressing,
    Why burdens can be blessings, Your love manifesting.

In moments of failure, when I fall short,
    And the lessons are hard, of every sort,
    Let me find the wisdom, in the trials I'm caressing,
    Why burdens can be blessings, Your grace expressing.

For every tribulation is a chance to grow,
    To show Your power, to let it flow,
    Through my struggles, let Your glory be pressing,
    Why burdens can be blessings, Your light undressing.

Help me to see beyond the pain,
    To the strength I gain, the love I attain,
    In every hardship, let me find the way,
    Why burdens can be blessings, each and every day.

Reflection

In this chapter, we're reminded that our burdens can be blessings in disguise. By understanding that our trials and struggles are opportunities for growth, strength, and wisdom, we can see God's love and grace manifest in our lives.

We learn to embrace our challenges, knowing that they build our character, perseverance, and hope. This chapter inspires us to find purpose in our pain and recognize that God is always at work, turning our burdens into blessings that reveal His glory.

Why Burdens Can Be Blessings

When We Look, What We Find

Understanding Burdens as Gifts

"In the journey of my life, with its ups and downs,
Through the smiles and the tears, the laughs and the frowns,
I seek to understand, with a heart that's confessing,
Why burdens can be blessings, Your gifts in disguise, impressing."

Bible Verse:

"Consider it pure joy, my brothers and sisters, whenever you face trials of many kinds, because you know that the testing of your faith produces perseverance." (James 1:2-3)

Inspirational Insight:

Context: James encourages believers to view trials as opportunities for growth and perseverance. This verse challenges us to find joy in our trials, understanding that they test and strengthen our faith. It aligns with the poem by suggesting that our burdens, though difficult, are gifts that help us grow and persevere.

Strength in Challenges

"When trials come my way, and the road gets tough,
And I feel overwhelmed, like I've had enough,
Help me see the strength, in each challenge I'm addressing,
Why burdens can be blessings, Your love manifesting."

Bible Verse:

"I can do all this through him who gives me strength." (Philippians 4:13)

Inspirational Insight:

Context: Paul emphasizes that we can endure all things through Christ who strengthens us. This verse reassures us that we can face any challenge with the strength God provides. It ties beautifully with the poem by reminding us that our burdens manifest God's love and strength in our lives, helping us to persevere.

Wisdom in Failures

"In moments of failure, when I fall short,
And the lessons are hard, of every sort,
Let me find the wisdom, in the trials I'm caressing,
Why burdens can be blessings, Your grace expressing."

Bible Verse:

"But he said to me, 'My grace is sufficient for you, for my power is made perfect in weakness.' Therefore I will boast all the more gladly about my weaknesses, so that Christ's power may rest on me." (2 Corinthians 12:9)

Inspirational Insight:

Context: Paul speaks of the sufficiency of God's grace and the strength found in our weaknesses. This verse highlights that God's grace is enough for us, and His power is made perfect in our weaknesses. It aligns with the poem by showing that even in our failures, we can find wisdom and experience God's grace, turning our burdens into blessings.

Growth Through Tribulations

"For every tribulation is a chance to grow,
To show Your power, to let it flow,

Why Burdens Can Be Blessings

Through my struggles, let Your glory be pressing,
Why burdens can be blessings, Your light undressing."

Bible Verse:
"Not only so, but we also glory in our sufferings, because we know that suffering produces perseverance; perseverance, character; and character, hope." (Romans 5:3-4)

Inspirational Insight:
Context: Paul explains that suffering leads to perseverance, character, and hope. This verse encourages us to see our sufferings as opportunities for growth. It ties back to the poem by emphasizing that our tribulations can reveal God's power and glory, transforming our burdens into blessings that build our character and hope.

Purpose in Pain
"Help me to see beyond the pain,
To the strength I gain, the love I attain,
In every hardship, let me find the way,
Why burdens can be blessings, each and every day."

Bible Verse:
"And we know that in all things God works for the good of those who love him, who have been called according to his purpose." (Romans 8:28)

Inspirational Insight:
Context: Paul reassures believers that God works all things for their good. This verse reminds us that God has a purpose for everything we go through, working all things for our

good. It aligns with the poem by encouraging us to look beyond our pain and recognize the strength and love we gain, understanding that our burdens can indeed be blessings.

Questions for Personal Reflection or Group Discussion

- How have you experienced growth or gained wisdom through your burdens?
- In what ways can you see God's love and grace manifesting in your challenges?
- How can you shift your perspective to view your burdens as opportunities for blessings?

Guided Prayer

- "Dear Lord, thank You for turning my burdens into blessings. Help me to see Your purpose in my struggles and to find strength, wisdom, and grace in every challenge. Amen."

Five

When God Asks for It Back

Welcome back and welcome to another chapter of our journey of faith and discovery. In this chapter, we'll explore the profound concept of surrendering everything back to God, recognizing that all we have is a gift from Him. Through poetry, scripture, and uplifting insights, we'll see how to live a life of gratitude, purpose, and readiness to return His blessings.

When God Asks for It Back

In the journey of life, with its twists and turns,
   Through the joys and the sorrows, the lessons learned,
   I acknowledge, with a heart that's not slack,
   Everything I have is His, when God asks for it back

All that I am, and all that I love,
   Are gifts from Him, from heaven above,

My Walk With Him

My life is on loan, a precious track,
   To live for His glory, when God asks for it back.

In moments of joy, and times of despair,
   In the laughter we share, and the burdens we bear,
   Let me be thankful, for the blessings that stack,
   And live to the fullest, when God asks for it back.

For every heartbeat, and every breath,
   Every sunrise, and every death,
   Are reminders that life is a fleeting knack,
   To cherish each moment, when God asks for it back.

Help me to live, with purpose and grace,
   To honor Your name, in every place,
   To express my gratitude, in all that I lack,
   And be ready to return it, when God asks for it back.

Reflection

In this chapter, we're reminded that everything we have is a gift from God, and we should live with a heart full of gratitude and readiness to return His blessings. By acknowledging God's ownership, living with purpose, embracing thankfulness, cherishing every moment, and surrendering with trust, we can honor Him in all we do.

This chapter inspires us to recognize the fleeting nature of life and to live each day fully, appreciating every blessing and being prepared to give it all back to God when He asks. It encourages us to trust in His plan and to live with grace and purpose, knowing that our lives are on loan from Him.

When We Look, What We Find

Acknowledging God's Ownership
"In the journey of life, with its twists and turns,
Through the joys and the sorrows, the lessons learned,
I acknowledge, with a heart that's not slack,
Everything I have is His, when God asks for it back."

Bible Verse:
"The earth is the Lord's, and everything in it, the world, and all who live in it." (Psalm 24:1)

Inspirational Insight:
Context: Psalm 24 acknowledges God's sovereignty over all creation. This verse reminds us that everything belongs to God, including our lives and possessions. It ties back to the poem by emphasizing the importance of recognizing God's ownership and being ready to return His gifts when He asks for them back.

Living with Gratitude and Purpose
"All that I am, and all that I love,
Are gifts from Him, from heaven above,
My life is on loan, a precious track,
To live for His glory, when God asks for it back."

Bible Verse:
"Whatever you do, work at it with all your heart, as working

for the Lord, not for human masters." (Colossians 3:23)

Inspirational Insight:
  Context: Paul encourages believers to work wholeheartedly for the Lord in all they do. This verse inspires us to live with purpose and gratitude, dedicating our efforts to God. It aligns with the poem by reminding us that our lives are on loan and should be lived for His glory, appreciating every moment as a gift from above.

Embracing Thankfulness in Joy and Sorrow
  "In moments of joy, and times of despair,
  In the laughter we share, and the burdens we bear,
  Let me be thankful, for the blessings that stack,
  And live to the fullest, when God asks for it back."

Bible Verse:
  "Give thanks in all circumstances; for this is God's will for you in Christ Jesus." (1 Thessalonians 5:18)

Inspirational Insight:
  Context: Paul advises believers to maintain a thankful heart in every situation. This verse encourages us to cultivate gratitude regardless of our circumstances. It ties beautifully with the poem by highlighting the importance of being thankful for both joys and sorrows, living fully and appreciatively, ready to return everything to God when He asks.

Cherishing Life's Fleeting Moments
  "For every heartbeat, and every breath,
  Every sunrise, and every death,

When God Asks for It Back

Are reminders that life is a fleeting knack,
To cherish each moment, when God asks for it back."

Bible Verse:
"Teach us to number our days, that we may gain a heart of wisdom." (Psalm 90:12)

Inspirational Insight:
Context: Moses prays for wisdom to appreciate the brevity of life. This verse urges us to value our time on earth and live wisely. It resonates with the poem by reminding us to cherish every moment, recognizing the fleeting nature of life and being prepared to return it all to God with a grateful heart.

Surrendering with Grace and Trust
"Help me to live, with purpose and grace,
To honor Your name, in every place,
To express my gratitude, in all that I lack,
And be ready to return it, when God asks for it back."

Bible Verse:
"Trust in the Lord with all your heart and lean not on your own understanding; in all your ways submit to him, and he will make your paths straight." (Proverbs 3:56)

Inspirational Insight:
Context: Proverbs encourages complete trust and submission to God's will. This verse calls us to trust God fully and surrender our lives to His guidance. It aligns with the poem by encouraging us to live purposefully and gratefully, always ready to return everything to God with trust in His perfect

My Walk With Him

plan.

Questions for Personal Reflection or Group Discussion

- How does recognizing that everything belongs to God change your perspective on life and possessions?
- In what ways can you live more purposefully and gratefully, acknowledging God's ownership?
- How can you prepare your heart to return everything to God with trust and grace?

Guided Prayer

- "Dear Lord, thank You for the blessings You have given me. Help me to live with a heart full of gratitude, purpose, and trust, always ready to return everything to You when You ask. Amen."

Six

When I Am Doing So Well, I Forget to Do Good

Hello again and welcome to another chapter of our journey of faith and discovery. In this chapter, we'll explore the importance of remembering to do good even when we are thriving. Through poetry, scripture, and uplifting insights, we'll see how to stay humble, compassionate, and focused on serving others, regardless of our personal success.

When I Am Doing So Well, I Forget to Do Good

When the sun shines bright on my path each day,
   And success comes easy, in every way,
   Let me not forget, in my life's parade,
   To stay humble and kind, in the good I've made.

When my cup overflows and my heart is light,

And everything seems to be going right,
Let me remember, in my prosperous mood,
To extend my hand and do some good.

When achievements pile high and accolades flow,
And the world seems to love the things I show,
Let me reflect Your love, in all that I do,
And never forget to be kind and true.

When life's going well and I'm on cloud nine,
And the blessings I have seem truly divine,
Let me serve others, with a heart that's pure,
To do good always, and be secure.

When my dreams come true and my goals are met,
And there's nothing more I could wish to get,
Let me keep Your commandments, with a heart so good,
To live in Your love, as I know I should.

Reflection

In this chapter, we're reminded of the importance of doing good even when we are thriving. By staying humble, practicing compassion, reflecting God's love, serving others with a grateful heart, and keeping God's commandments, we can ensure that our success does not lead us away from our purpose.

This chapter inspires us to use our blessings as opportunities to bless others, maintaining a heart of kindness and service. It encourages us to remember that true success is not just in

When I Am Doing So Well, I Forget to Do Good

what we achieve but in how we use our achievements to make a positive impact on the world around us.

When We Look, What We Find

Staying Humble in Success
"When the sun shines bright on my path each day,
And success comes easy, in every way,
Let me not forget, in my life's parade,
To stay humble and kind, in the good I've made."

Bible Verse:
"Do nothing out of selfish ambition or vain conceit. Rather, in humility value others above yourselves." (Philippians 2:3)

Inspirational Insight:
Context: Paul encourages believers to practice humility and consider others more significant than themselves. This verse serves as a gentle reminder to remain humble and considerate, even when we are successful. It ties back to the poem by emphasizing the importance of valuing others and staying grounded, ensuring that our success does not lead us to forget the good we can do for others.

Practicing Compassion Amidst Prosperity
"When my cup overflows and my heart is light,
And everything seems to be going right,
Let me remember, in my prosperous mood,
To extend my hand and do some good."

Bible Verse:

"Command them to do good, to be rich in good deeds, and to be generous and willing to share." (1 Timothy 6:18)

Inspirational Insight:
Context: Paul advises the wealthy to be generous and to focus on doing good deeds. This verse encourages us to use our prosperity as an opportunity to be generous and perform good deeds. It aligns with the poem by reminding us that when we are doing well, we should not forget to extend our blessings to others through acts of kindness and compassion.

Reflecting God's Love Through Actions
"When achievements pile high and accolades flow,
And the world seems to love the things I show,
Let me reflect Your love, in all that I do,
And never forget to be kind and true."

Bible Verse:
"In the same way, let your light shine before others, that they may see your good deeds and glorify your Father in heaven." (Matthew 5:16)
Inspirational Insight:

Context: Jesus encourages His followers to let their good deeds shine to glorify God. This verse calls us to let our actions reflect God's love and bring glory to Him. It ties beautifully with the poem by emphasizing that our success should be a platform to showcase kindness and goodness, ensuring that our deeds point others to God's love and grace.

Serving Others with a Grateful Heart

When I Am Doing So Well, I Forget to Do Good

"When life's going well and I'm on cloud nine,
And the blessings I have seem truly divine,
Let me serve others, with a heart that's pure,
To do good always, and be secure."

Bible Verse:
"Each of you should use whatever gift you have received to serve others, as faithful stewards of God's grace in its various forms." (1 Peter 4:10)

Inspirational Insight:
Context: Peter encourages believers to use their gifts to serve others faithfully. This verse reminds us that our gifts and blessings are meant to be used in service to others. It aligns with the poem by encouraging us to serve with a grateful heart, ensuring that our success and blessings lead us to acts of goodness and service.

Keeping God's Commandments in Prosperity
"When my dreams come true and my goals are met,
And there's nothing more I could wish to get,
Let me keep Your commandments, with a heart so good,
To live in Your love, as I know I should."

Bible Verse:
"If you love me, keep my commands." (John 14:15)

Inspirational Insight:
Context: Jesus emphasizes the importance of keeping His commandments as an expression of love. This verse highlights that our love for God is demonstrated through our obedience

My Walk With Him

to His commands. It ties back to the poem by reminding us to remain faithful to God's teachings, ensuring that our success does not lead us away from His path but rather strengthens our commitment to doing good.

Questions for Personal Reflection or Group Discussion

- How can you stay humble and grounded during times of success?
- In what ways can you use your prosperity to extend kindness and compassion to others?
- How can you ensure that your actions reflect God's love and bring glory to Him?

Guided Prayer

- "Dear Lord, thank You for the blessings and success in my life. Help me to stay humble, compassionate, and focused on doing good, reflecting Your love in all that I do. Amen."

Seven

Please, I'm Sorry and Thank You

Hey there! Welcome to another chapter of our journey of faith and discovery. In this chapter, we'll delve into the powerful trio of words: "Please," "I'm Sorry," and "Thank you." Through poetry, scripture, and uplifting insights, we'll explore how these expressions of humility, repentance, and gratitude can transform our relationships with God and others.

Please, I'm Sorry and Thank You

In the quiet of my heart, I humbly pray,
   With a plea for guidance, each passing day,
   I seek Your wisdom, with a soul at ease,
   And whisper softly, my heartfelt 'Please.

In moments of weakness, when I've gone astray,
   With a heart contrite, I come to pray,

Seeking forgiveness, on bended knee,
I utter softly, 'I'm Sorry.'

For the blessings seen, and those unseen,
   For the grace that flows, so pure and clean,
   With a grateful heart, in all I do,
I lift my voice and say, 'Thank You.'

In my interactions, both great and small,
   Let humility guide, in each and all,
   With 'Please,' 'I'm Sorry,' and 'Thank You' true,
I build connections, strong and new.

In every moment, through joy and strife,
   Let these words be the rhythm of my life,
   With grace and love, in all I pursue,
I live by 'Please,' 'I'm Sorry,' and 'Thank You.'

Reflection

In this chapter, we're reminded of the transformative power of "Please," "I'm Sorry," and "Thank You." By incorporating these expressions into our daily lives, we can deepen our relationship with God and strengthen our connections with others.

This chapter inspires us to approach God and others with humility, seek forgiveness with sincerity, and express gratitude with a thankful heart. It encourages us to live a life marked by grace, kindness, and respect, using these powerful words to build a more loving and compassionate world.

Please, I'm Sorry and Thank You

When We Look, What We Find

The Power of "Please"
"In the quiet of my heart, I humbly pray,
With a plea for guidance, each passing day,
I seek Your wisdom, with a soul at ease,
And whisper softly, my heartfelt 'Please.'"

Bible Verse:
"Ask and it will be given to you; seek and you will find; knock and the door will be opened to you." (Matthew 7:7)

Inspirational Insight:
Context: Jesus encourages His followers to ask, seek, and knock, promising that God will respond. This verse reassures us that God is attentive to our requests and encourages us to approach Him with our needs. It aligns with the poem by reminding us of the power of humbly asking God for guidance and help, trusting that He listens and responds to our please.

The Healing of "I'm Sorry"
"In moments of weakness, when I've gone astray,
With a heart contrite, I come to pray,
Seeking forgiveness, on bended knee,
I utter softly, 'I'm Sorry.'"

Bible Verse:
"If we confess our sins, he is faithful and just and will forgive us our sins and purify us from all unrighteousness." (1 John 1:9)

Inspirational Insight:

Context: John assures believers of God's faithfulness in forgiving confessed sins. This verse offers the comforting promise of God's forgiveness when we confess our wrongdoings. It ties beautifully with the poem by highlighting the healing power of repentance and the importance of seeking God's forgiveness with a sincere heart.

The Gratitude in "Thank You"
"For the blessings seen, and those unseen,
For the grace that flows, so pure and clean,
With a grateful heart, in all I do,
I lift my voice and say, 'Thank You.'"

Bible Verse:

"Give thanks to the Lord, for he is good; his love endures forever." (Psalm 107:1)

Inspirational Insight:

Context: This Psalm encourages believers to express gratitude for God's enduring love and goodness. This verse invites us to cultivate a spirit of gratitude, recognizing God's goodness and everlasting love. It aligns with the poem by reminding us to always give thanks, appreciating both the visible and invisible blessings in our lives.

Strengthening Relationships with Humility
"In my interactions, both great and small,
Let humility guide, in each and all,
With 'Please,' 'I'm Sorry,' and 'Thank You' true,
I build connections, strong and new."

Please, I'm Sorry and Thank You

Bible Verse:
"Be completely humble and gentle; be patient, bearing with one another in love." (Ephesians 4:2)

Inspirational Insight:
Context: Paul advises believers to practice humility, gentleness, and patience in their relationships. This verse emphasizes the importance of humility and patience in fostering loving relationships. It ties back to the poem by encouraging us to use "Please," "I'm Sorry," and "Thank You" to build and strengthen our connections with others, demonstrating love and respect.

Living a Life of Grace
"In every moment, through joy and strife,
Let these words be the rhythm of my life,
With grace and love, in all I pursue,
I live by 'Please,' 'I'm Sorry,' and 'Thank You.'"

Bible Verse:
"Let your conversation be always full of grace, seasoned with salt, so that you may know how to answer everyone." (Colossians 4:6)

Inspirational Insight:
Context: Paul encourages believers to speak with grace and wisdom. This verse calls us to infuse our speech with grace and thoughtfulness. It resonates with the poem by highlighting how "Please," "I'm Sorry," and "Thank You" can guide us in living a life marked by grace, kindness, and wisdom.

Questions for Personal Reflection or Group Discussion

My Walk With Him

- How can you incorporate "Please," "I'm Sorry," and "Thank You" more intentionally in your daily interactions?
- In what ways can these expressions of humility, repentance, and gratitude transform your relationships with God and others?
- How can you cultivate a heart of gratitude and a spirit of humility in all you do?

Guided Prayer

- "Dear Lord, thank You for the blessings You have given me. Help me to approach You and others with humility, seek forgiveness sincerely, and express my gratitude wholeheartedly. May 'Please,' 'I'm Sorry,' and 'Thank You' be the rhythm of my life. Amen."

Eight

Less Like Me and More Like You

Hello! Welcome to another chapter of our journey of faith and discovery. In this chapter, we'll explore the profound desire to become less like ourselves and more like Christ. Through poetry, scripture, and uplifting insights, we'll see how to cultivate Christ-like qualities in our lives, allowing His love, humility, and grace to shine through us.

Less Like Me and More Like You

In the quiet of my heart, a prayer I raise,
   To be transformed by Your loving ways,
   Less of my will, and more of Your view,
   Make me less like me, and more like You.

Teach me humility, as You showed on the cross,
   To serve with love, no matter the cost,

My Walk With Him

In every action, in all that I do,
Let me be less like me, and more like You.

Fill my heart with compassion, pure and true,
   To love as You love, in all that I pursue,
   Let Your light shine through, in all I do,
   Make me less like me, and more like You.

Guide my steps, Lord, in Your perfect way,
   To follow Your will, each and every day,
   In surrender and trust, my heart renew,
   Make me less like me, and more like You.

Let Your grace flow through me, in word and deed,
   To forgive as You forgive, in times of need,
   In every moment, help me to pursue,
   Being less like me, and more like You.

Reflection

In this chapter, we're reminded of the profound desire to become less like ourselves and more like Christ. By embracing humility, radiating Christ's love, seeking God's will, and reflecting His grace and forgiveness, we can transform our lives to mirror His character.

This chapter inspires us to cultivate Christ-like qualities, allowing His love and grace to shine through us. It encourages us to surrender our own desires and will, seeking to live a life that reflects His love, humility, and compassion in all that we do.

Less Like Me and More Like You

When We Look, What We Find

The Desire for Transformation
  "In the quiet of my heart, a prayer I raise,
  To be transformed by Your loving ways,
  Less of my will, and more of Your view,
  Make me less like me, and more like You."

Bible Verse:
  "Therefore, if anyone is in Christ, the new creation has come: The old has gone, the new is here!" (2 Corinthians 5:17)

Inspirational Insight:
  Context: Paul speaks about the transformative power of being in Christ, becoming a new creation. This verse reminds us that in Christ, we are made new, shedding our old selves. It aligns with the poem by emphasizing the desire for transformation, seeking to become more like Christ in our thoughts, actions, and character.

Embracing Humility and Service
  "Teach me humility, as You showed on the cross,
  To serve with love, no matter the cost,
  In every action, in all that I do,
  Let me be less like me, and more like You."

Bible Verse:
  "Do nothing out of selfish ambition or vain conceit. Rather, in humility value others above yourselves." (Philippians 2:3)

Inspirational Insight:

Context: Paul encourages believers to practice humility and consider others more significant than themselves. This verse calls us to embrace humility and selflessness, valuing others above ourselves. It ties beautifully with the poem by highlighting the importance of serving others with Christ-like love and humility, striving to reflect His character in our lives.

Radiating Christ's Love
"Fill my heart with compassion, pure and true,
To love as You love, in all that I pursue,
Let Your light shine through, in all I do,
Make me less like me, and more like You."

Bible Verse:
"A new command I give you: Love one another. As I have loved you, so you must love one another." (John 13:34)

Inspirational Insight:
Context: Jesus commands His followers to love one another as He has loved them. This verse emphasizes the importance of loving others with the same selfless love that Jesus demonstrated. It aligns with the poem by encouraging us to let Christ's love fill our hearts and guide our actions, making us more like Him in our relationships and interactions.

Seeking God's Will
"Guide my steps, Lord, in Your perfect way,
To follow Your will, each and every day,
In surrender and trust, my heart renew,
Make me less like me, and more like You."

Less Like Me and More Like You

Bible Verse:
"Trust in the Lord with all your heart and lean not on your own understanding; in all your ways submit to him, and he will make your paths straight." (Proverbs 3:5-6)

Inspirational Insight:
Context: This proverb encourages believers to trust in God's wisdom and guidance. This verse calls us to trust and submit to God's will, acknowledging His wisdom over our own understanding. It ties back to the poem by emphasizing the importance of seeking God's guidance and allowing His will to shape our lives, making us more like Christ.

Reflecting Christ's Grace and Forgiveness
"Let Your grace flow through me, in word and deed,
To forgive as You forgive, in times of need,
In every moment, help me to pursue,
Being less like me, and more like You."

Bible Verse:
"Be kind and compassionate to one another, forgiving each other, just as in Christ God forgave you." (Ephesians 4:32)

Inspirational Insight:
Context: Paul encourages believers to practice kindness, compassion, and forgiveness. This verse reminds us to embody Christ's grace and forgiveness in our interactions with others. It aligns with the poem by encouraging us to reflect Christ's character through our actions, striving to be kind, compassionate, and forgiving.

My Walk With Him

Questions for Personal Reflection or Group Discussion

- In what areas of your life do you feel called to become more like Christ?
- How can you practice humility and selflessness in your daily interactions?
- What steps can you take to seek God's will and guidance more intentionally?

Guided Prayer

- "Dear Lord, thank You for the example of Jesus Christ. Help me to become less like myself and more like Him. Fill my heart with His love, humility, and grace, and guide my steps according to Your will. Amen."

Nine

Why "No" May Be the Best Answer

Hey there! Welcome to another chapter of our journey of faith and discovery. In this chapter, we'll explore the profound wisdom in understanding why "No" may sometimes be the best answer from God. Through poetry, scripture, and uplifting insights, we'll see how to trust God's plan, recognizing that His "No" can be a pathway to greater blessings and growth.

Why "No" May Be the Best Answer

When my heart desires and my hopes are high,
   And I lift my prayers to the sky,
     Though my plans may seem so right,
     God's 'No' may guide me to His light.

In the waiting and the wondering why,
   When the answer is a gentle 'No,'

My Walk With Him

I'll trust in Your perfect timing,
   For You know the way I should go.

In the moments of refusal,
   When my plans fall through,
   I learn to lean on Your wisdom,
   And find strength anew.

When doors close and dreams fade,
   And I face a 'No' in life's parade,
   I'll trust You're redirecting me,
   To blessings greater than I can see.

In the quiet of acceptance,
   When I surrender to Your will,
   I find peace in Your 'No,'
   And my heart is still.

Reflection

In this chapter, we're reminded of the profound wisdom in understanding why "No" may sometimes be the best answer from God. By trusting His wisdom, embracing His timing, learning through denial, and finding peace in His plan, we can grow in faith and experience greater blessings.

This chapter inspires us to see God's "No" not as a rejection, but as a redirection towards His perfect plan for our lives. It encourages us to trust in His greater wisdom and timing, knowing that He works all things for our good.

Why "No" May Be the Best Answer

When We Look, What We Find

Trusting God's Wisdom
"When my heart desires and my hopes are high,
And I lift my prayers to the sky,
Though my plans may seem so right,
God's 'No' may guide me to His light."

Bible Verse:
"For my thoughts are not your thoughts, neither are your ways my ways," declares the Lord. (Isaiah 55:8)

Inspirational Insight:
Context: God speaks through Isaiah, reminding us that His thoughts and ways are higher than ours. This verse reassures us that God's wisdom surpasses our understanding. It aligns with the poem by emphasizing the importance of trusting God's perspective, even when His answer is "No," knowing that He sees the bigger picture and has our best interests at heart.

Embracing God's Timing
"In the waiting and the wondering why,
When the answer is a gentle 'No,'
I'll trust in Your perfect timing,
For You know the way I should go."

Bible Verse:
"He has made everything beautiful in its time." (Ecclesiastes 3:11)

Inspirational Insight:

Context: The author of Ecclesiastes reflects on the beauty of God's timing. This verse encourages us to trust in God's perfect timing, knowing that He makes everything beautiful in its own time. It ties beautifully with the poem by reminding us that a "No" today may lead to a more beautiful and timely "Yes" in the future.

Learning Through Denial
"In the moments of refusal,
When my plans fall through,
I learn to lean on Your wisdom,
And find strength anew."

Bible Verse:
"Consider it pure joy, my brothers and sisters, whenever you face trials of many kinds, because you know that the testing of your faith produces perseverance." (James 1:2-3)

Inspirational Insight:
Context: James encourages believers to find joy in trials, recognizing their role in producing perseverance. This verse highlights the growth that comes from facing challenges and denials. It aligns with the poem by emphasizing that God's "No" can be a tool for building our faith and perseverance, leading us to greater spiritual maturity.

Redirecting to Greater Blessings
"When doors close and dreams fade,
And I face a 'No' in life's parade,
I'll trust You're redirecting me,
To blessings greater than I can see."

Why "No" May Be the Best Answer

Bible Verse:
"And we know that in all things God works for the good of those who love him, who have been called according to his purpose." (Romans 8:28)

Inspirational Insight:
Context: Paul reassures believers that God works all things for their good. This verse offers the comforting promise that God orchestrates everything for our good. It ties back to the poem by reminding us that a "No" can be God's way of redirecting us to greater blessings and fulfilling His purpose in our lives.

Finding Peace in God's Plan
"In the quiet of acceptance,
When I surrender to Your will,
I find peace in Your 'No,'
And my heart is still."

Bible Verse:
"And the peace of God, which transcends all understanding, will guard your hearts and your minds in Christ Jesus." (Philippians 4:7)

Inspirational Insight:
Context: Paul speaks about the peace of God that surpasses understanding. This verse highlights the peace that comes from trusting in God's plan. It aligns with the poem by encouraging us to find tranquility in God's "No," knowing that His peace will guard our hearts and minds as we trust in Him.

My Walk With Him

Questions for Personal Reflection or Group Discussion

- How do you typically respond when God's answer is "No"?
- In what ways can you learn to trust God's wisdom and timing more deeply?
- Can you recall a time when a "No" from God led to a greater blessing or growth in your life?

Guided Prayer

- "Dear Lord, thank You for Your wisdom and guidance. Help me to trust in Your perfect plan, even when the answer is 'No.' Grant me the peace to accept Your will and the faith to believe that You are working all things for my good. Amen."

Ten

The Power of Forgiveness

Welcome to another chapter in our journey of faith and personal growth. In this chapter, we'll explore the transformative power of forgiveness. Through poetry, scripture, and uplifting insights, we'll discover how forgiveness can heal our hearts, restore relationships, and bring us closer to God's love and grace.

The Power of Forgiveness

Bitterness weighs, a heavy chain,
   Holding my heart in silent pain,
   But in forgiveness, I find release,
   A path to freedom and inner peace.

As Christ forgave, so must I,
   To mirror His love from on high,

In pardoning others, I find,
God's grace reflected in my mind.

In letting go of hurt and pain,
I find my soul can breathe again,
Forgiveness heals the deepest part,
And mends the fractures in my heart.

Though memories linger, sharp and clear,
I choose to forgive, year after year,
Not for their sake, but for my own,
To free my heart and make it whole.

In forgiving, I set a prisoner free,
Only to discover that prisoner was me,
In this act of grace, I come to see,
The love of God, setting my spirit free.

Reflection

In this chapter, we've explored the transformative power of forgiveness. We've seen how forgiveness can free us from the weight of bitterness, reflect God's grace in our lives, heal our emotional wounds, and liberate our spirits. Forgiveness is not always easy, but it's a choice that brings us closer to God's love and the freedom He intends for us.

This chapter encourages us to embrace forgiveness as a way of life, recognizing it as a powerful tool for personal growth, relational healing, and spiritual maturity. By choosing to forgive, we align ourselves with God's heart and experience the profound peace and freedom that comes from letting go of hurt and embracing grace.

When We Look, What We Find

The Weight of Unforgiveness
"Bitterness weighs, a heavy chain,
Holding my heart in silent pain,
But in forgiveness, I find release,
A path to freedom and inner peace."

Bible Verse:
"Get rid of all bitterness, rage and anger, brawling and slander, along with every form of malice." (Ephesians 4:31)

Inspirational Insight:
Context: Paul advises the Ephesians to let go of negative emotions that hinder spiritual growth. : This verse highlights the importance of releasing bitterness and anger. It aligns with the poem by emphasizing how unforgiveness can weigh us down, while forgiveness offers a path to freedom and peace.

Forgiveness as a Divine Example
"As Christ forgave, so must I,
To mirror His love from on high,
In pardoning others, I find,
God's grace reflected in my mind."

Bible Verse:
"Bear with each other and forgive one another if any of you has a grievance against someone. Forgive as the Lord forgave

you." (Colossians 3:13)

Inspirational Insight:
  Context: Paul encourages believers to forgive others as Christ has forgiven them. This verse reminds us that our ability to forgive is rooted in God's forgiveness of us. It ties beautifully with the poem by showing how our act of forgiving others reflects God's grace in our lives.

Healing Through Forgiveness
  "In letting go of hurt and pain,
  I find my soul can breathe again,
  Forgiveness heals the deepest part,
  And mends the fractures in my heart."

Bible Verse:
  "He heals the brokenhearted and binds up their wounds." (Psalm 147:3)

Inspirational Insight:
  Context: The psalmist praises God for His healing power. This verse speaks to God's ability to heal our emotional wounds. It aligns with the poem by highlighting how forgiveness can be a powerful tool for emotional and spiritual healing.

Forgiveness as a Choice
  "Though memories linger, sharp and clear,
  I choose to forgive, year after year,
  Not for their sake, but for my own,
  To free my heart and make it whole."

The Power of Forgiveness

Bible Verse:
"For if you forgive other people when they sin against you, your heavenly Father will also forgive you." (Matthew 6:14)

Inspirational Insight:
Context: Jesus teaches about the importance of forgiveness in the Lord's Prayer. This verse emphasizes that forgiveness is a choice we make, with spiritual consequences. It ties back to the poem by showing that forgiveness is an ongoing process that benefits the forgiver as much as the forgiven.

The Liberating Power of Forgiveness
"In forgiving, I set a prisoner free,
Only to discover that prisoner was me,
In this act of grace, I come to see,
The love of God, setting my spirit free."

Bible Verse:
"It is for freedom that Christ has set us free. Stand firm, then, and do not let yourselves be burdened again by a yoke of slavery." (Galatians 5:1)

Inspirational Insight:
Context: Paul speaks about the freedom Christ offers from the bondage of sin. While this verse speaks broadly about spiritual freedom, it can be applied to the freedom that comes from forgiveness. It aligns with the poem by illustrating how forgiveness liberates us from the bondage of resentment and bitterness.

Questions for Personal Reflection or Group Discussion

My Walk With Him

- What areas of your life might be burdened by unforgiveness?
- How has God's forgiveness impacted your ability to forgive others?
- Can you recall a time when choosing to forgive brought healing or freedom to your life?

Guided Prayer

- "Heavenly Father, thank You for Your endless forgiveness and grace. Help me to forgive as You have forgiven me. Give me the strength to let go of bitterness and embrace the freedom that comes through forgiveness. May Your love flow through me as I extend grace to others. Amen."

Eleven

On a Different Road

Hey there! Welcome to another chapter of our journey of faith and personal growth. In this chapter, we'll explore the idea of being led down a different road than we originally planned. Through poetry, scripture, and uplifting insights, we'll discover how God's redirection can lead us to unexpected blessings and deeper trust in His divine plan.

On a Different Road

When my path takes an unexpected turn,
   And familiar plans begin to burn,
   I trust in Your guiding hand,
   Leading me to a promised land.

In the midst of change and new unknowns,
   I find Your purpose gently shown,

A different road, yet guided by grace,
Leading me to a sacred place.

When the road ahead seems unclear,
   And doubts and fears draw near,
   I lean on Your wisdom, steadfast and true,
   Trusting the path You've chosen, anew.

On this new road, I find surprise,
   Blessings hidden in disguise,
   With each step, my faith renewed,
   I see Your promises, all come true.

Though the road is different than I planned,
   I walk with faith, guided by Your hand,
   With strength renewed, and courage bold,
   I trust in Your story, yet untold.

Reflection

In this chapter, we've explored the idea of being led down a different road than we originally planned. We've seen how God's redirection can lead to unexpected blessings, deeper trust, and a stronger faith. Embracing divine detours, finding purpose in redirection, and trusting in God's plan can transform our journey into one of discovery and growth.

This chapter encourages us to see changes in our path not as setbacks, but as opportunities to experience God's guidance and blessings in new ways. By trusting in His wisdom and embracing the journey, we can find joy and fulfillment on roads we never imagined.

When We Look, What We Find

Embracing Divine Detours
"When my path takes an unexpected turn,
And familiar plans begin to burn,
I trust in Your guiding hand,
Leading me to a promised land."

Bible Verse:
"In their hearts humans plan their course, but the Lord establishes their steps." (Proverbs 16:9)

Inspirational Insight:
Context: This proverb contrasts human plans and God's sovereign guidance. This verse reassures us that while we may make our own plans, God ultimately directs our steps. It aligns with the poem by emphasizing the importance of trusting God when our path changes unexpectedly, believing that He is leading us to His greater purpose.

Finding Purpose in Redirection
"In the midst of change and new unknowns,
I find Your purpose gently shown,
A different road, yet guided by grace,
Leading me to a sacred place."

Bible Verse:
"And we know that in all things God works for the good of those who love him, who have been called according to his

purpose." (Romans 8:28)

Inspirational Insight:

Context: Paul assures believers that God works all things for their good and His purpose. This verse offers the comforting promise that God orchestrates everything for our good. It ties beautifully with the poem by reminding us that even when we are redirected, God's purpose is at work, leading us to places of blessing and growth.

Trusting in God's Plan
"When the road ahead seems unclear,
And doubts and fears draw near,
I lean on Your wisdom, steadfast and true,
Trusting the path You've chosen, anew."

Bible Verse:
"Trust in the Lord with all your heart and lean not on your own understanding; in all your ways submit to him, and he will make your paths straight." (Proverbs 3:5-6)

Inspirational Insight:

Context: This proverb encourages complete trust in God's wisdom and guidance. This verse calls us to trust God wholeheartedly and not rely on our own understanding. It aligns with the poem by emphasizing the importance of submitting to God's plan, especially when the road ahead is uncertain.

The Blessings of New Paths
"On this new road, I find surprise,

On a Different Road

Blessings hidden in disguise,
With each step, my faith renewed,
I see Your promises, all come true."

Bible Verse:
"For I know the plans I have for you," declares the Lord, "plans to prosper you and not to harm you, plans to give you hope and a future." (Jeremiah 29:11)

Inspirational Insight:
Context: God speaks through Jeremiah to assure the Israelites of His good plans for their future. This verse reassures us of God's good intentions for our lives. It ties back to the poem by highlighting how new paths, though unexpected, can lead to surprising blessings and the fulfillment of God's promises.

Strength in God's Guidance
"Though the road is different than I planned,
I walk with faith, guided by Your hand,
With strength renewed, and courage bold,
I trust in Your story, yet untold."

Bible Verse:
"The Lord makes firm the steps of the one who delights in him; though he may stumble, he will not fall, for the Lord upholds him with his hand." (Psalm 37:23-24)

Inspirational Insight:
Context: The psalmist speaks about God's steadfast support for those who follow Him. This verse highlights God's

unwavering support and guidance. It aligns with the poem by emphasizing that even when we face challenges on a different road, God upholds us and strengthens our steps.

Questions for Personal Reflection or Group Discussion

- How do you typically respond when your plans change unexpectedly?
- Can you recall a time when being led down a different road resulted in unexpected blessings?
- How can you cultivate a deeper trust in God's guidance and plan for your life?

Guided Prayer

- "Dear Lord, thank You for guiding my steps, even when the road is different than I planned. Help me to trust in Your wisdom and embrace the journey You've set before me. Strengthen my faith and renew my courage as I walk with You. Amen."

Twelve

Living on Borrowed Grace

Welcome to another chapter in our journey of faith and discovery. In this chapter, we'll explore the concept of living on borrowed grace. Through poetry, scripture, and uplifting insights, we'll discover how God's grace sustains us daily, even when we feel unworthy or incapable. We'll learn to rely on His grace, recognizing it as the foundation of our spiritual journey and the source of our strength.

Living on Borrowed Grace

In the quiet moments, I feel Your embrace,
   A gift unearned, Your boundless grace,
   Though unworthy, I find my place,
   Living each day on borrowed grace.

In my weakness, Your strength is found,

Lifting me up from the ground,
When I falter, in Your love I'm bound,
Living on Your grace, where hope is crowned.

In every trial, in every need,
Your grace supplies, Your love proceeds,
With every step, Your Spirit leads,
Living on Your grace, my soul concedes.

When I stumble and lose my way,
Your grace forgives, come what may,
In Your mercy, I choose to stay,
Living on Your grace, day by day.

Transforming hearts, renewing minds,
Your grace redeems, Your love refines,
In Your presence, true life I find,
Living on Your grace, forever entwined.

Reflection

In this chapter, we've delved into the concept of living on borrowed grace. We've seen how God's grace is a gift that sustains us, empowers us in our weaknesses, meets our every need, forgives us, and transforms us. Living on borrowed grace means recognizing our dependence on God's unmerited favor and allowing it to shape our lives.

This chapter encourages us to embrace grace as the foundation of our spiritual journey, trusting in its sufficiency and transformative power. By living on borrowed grace, we acknowledge our need for God and experience the fullness of His love and provision.

When We Look, What We Find

The Gift of Grace
"In the quiet moments, I feel Your embrace,
A gift unearned, Your boundless grace,
Though unworthy, I find my place,
Living each day on borrowed grace."

Bible Verse:
"For it is by grace you have been saved, through faith—and this is not from yourselves, it is the gift of God." (Ephesians 2:8)

Inspirational Insight:
Context: Paul emphasizes that salvation is a gift of grace from God, not earned by works. This verse reminds us that grace is a divine gift, freely given by God. It aligns with the poem by highlighting the unearned nature of grace and our dependence on it for salvation and daily living.

Your Grace in Our Weakness
"In my weakness, Your strength is found,
Lifting me up from the ground,
When I falter, in Your love I'm bound,
Living on grace, where hope is crowned."

Bible Verse:
"But he said to me, 'My grace is sufficient for you, for my

power is made perfect in weakness.'" (2 Corinthians 12:9)

Inspirational Insight:

Context: Paul shares God's assurance that His grace is sufficient, especially in times of weakness. This verse reassures us that God's grace is sufficient to carry us through our weaknesses. It ties beautifully with the poem by emphasizing how God's grace empowers us and becomes our strength when we are weak.

Grace for Every Need
"In every trial, in every need,
Your grace supplies, Your love proceeds,
With every step, Your Spirit leads,
Living on grace, my soul concedes."

Bible Verse:
"And God can bless you abundantly, so that in all things at all times, having all that you need, you will abound in every good work." (2 Corinthians 9:8)

Inspirational Insight:

Context: Paul speaks about God's ability to provide abundantly for every need. This verse highlights God's provision through His grace, ensuring we have all we need to abound in good works. It aligns with the poem by showing how God's grace meets our every need and guides us in our daily lives.

Grace in Forgiveness
"When I stumble and lose my way,
Your grace forgives, come what may,

Living on Borrowed Grace

In Your mercy, I choose to stay,
Living on grace, day by day."

Bible Verse:
"In him we have redemption through his blood, the forgiveness of sins, in accordance with the riches of God's grace." (Ephesians 1:7)

Inspirational Insight:
Context: Paul speaks about the redemption and forgiveness we receive through Christ's sacrifice. This verse underscores the forgiveness we receive through God's grace. It ties back to the poem by illustrating how grace continually forgives and redeems us, allowing us to live each day in the light of His mercy.

Grace That Transforms
"Transforming hearts, renewing minds,
Your grace redeems, Your love refines,
In Your presence, true life I find,
Living on grace, forever entwined."

Bible Verse:
"Do not conform to the pattern of this world, but be transformed by the renewing of your mind. Then you will be able to test and approve what God's will is—his good, pleasing and perfect will." (Romans 12:2)

Inspirational Insight:
Context: Paul encourages believers to be transformed by renewing their minds through God's grace. This verse speaks

to the transformative power of God's grace in renewing our minds and aligning us with His will. It aligns with the poem by highlighting how grace changes us from the inside out, refining us and drawing us closer to God.

Questions for Personal Reflection or Group Discussion

- How have you experienced God's grace in your life?
- How can you rely more on God's grace in your daily struggles and weaknesses?
- How does understanding grace as a gift influence your relationship with God and others?

Guided Prayer

- "Dear Lord, thank You for Your boundless grace that sustains me daily. Help me to live fully in the light of Your grace, trusting in Your provision and strength. Transform my heart and mind, and let Your grace guide me. Amen."

Thirteen

He Was Holding My Hand

~~~

Hello! Welcome to another chapter in our journey of faith and discovery. In this chapter, we'll explore the comforting and reassuring presence of God in our lives. Through poetry, scripture, and uplifting insights, we'll discover how God holds our hand through every trial and triumph, offering us His unwavering support and love.

He Was Holding My Hand

In the darkest night, when fears arise,
  I feel Your hand, a calming guise,
    Through every storm, in every land,
  I know, my God, You hold my hand.

When paths are unclear, and I cannot see,
  Your hand guides, gently leading me,

My Walk With Him

Through twists and turns, I understand,
My steps are sure, You hold my hand.

When my strength fails and hope seems thin,
Your hand lifts me, from deep within,
In weakness, I find strength so grand,
For in my trials, You hold my hand.

In joy or sorrow, loss or gain,
Your love remains, a constant refrain,
Through every season, by Your plan,
I'm never alone, You hold my hand.

With every step, in faith I stand,
Knowing always, You hold my hand,
Through life's journey, near or far,
My guiding light, my morning star.

Reflection

In this chapter, we've explored the comforting reality that God holds our hand through every aspect of life. We've seen how His presence brings comfort, guidance, strength, assurance, and direction. Knowing that God holds our hand reassures us that we are never alone and that His love and support are constant.

This chapter encourages us to trust in God's hand, especially in moments of uncertainty and weakness. By recognizing His presence and relying on His guidance, we can navigate life's challenges with confidence and peace.

He Was Holding My Hand

When We Look, What We Find

The Comfort of His Presence
"In the darkest night, when fears arise,
I feel Your hand, a calming guise,
Through every storm, in every land,
I know, my God, You hold my hand."

Bible Verse:
"Even though I walk through the darkest valley, I will fear no evil, for you are with me; your rod and your staff, they comfort me." (Psalm 23:4)

Inspirational Insight:
Context: David expresses his confidence in God's presence and protection even in the darkest times. This verse reassures us of God's comforting presence during our toughest moments. It aligns with the poem by emphasizing how God's hand holds and guides us through life's challenges, providing comfort and courage.

His Guidance in Uncertainty
"When paths are unclear, and I cannot see,
Your hand guides, gently leading me,
Through twists and turns, I understand,
My steps are sure, You hold my hand."

Bible Verse:
"I will instruct you and teach you in the way you should go; I will counsel you with my loving eye on you." (Psalm 32:8)

Inspirational Insight:
Context: God promises guidance and instruction to those who trust in Him. This verse highlights God's commitment to guiding us through life's uncertainties. It ties beautifully with the poem by showing that even when our path is unclear, God's hand leads us with love and wisdom.

Strength in Times of Weakness
"When my strength fails and hope seems thin,
Your hand lifts me, from deep within,
In weakness, I find strength so grand,
For in my trials, You hold my hand."

Bible Verse:
"So do not fear, for I am with you; do not be dismayed, for I am your God. I will strengthen you and help you; I will uphold you with my righteous right hand." (Isaiah 41:10)

Inspirational Insight:
Context: God assures His people of His presence, strength, and support. This verse provides a powerful reminder of God's promise to strengthen and uphold us. It aligns with the poem by emphasizing that in our moments of weakness, God's hand is there to lift and support us.

Assurance of His Love
"In joy or sorrow, loss or gain,
Your love remains, a constant refrain,
Through every season, by Your plan,
I'm never alone, You hold my hand."

He Was Holding My Hand

Bible Verse:

"For I am convinced that neither death nor life, neither angels nor demons, neither the present nor the future, nor any powers, neither height nor depth, nor anything else in all creation, will be able to separate us from the love of God that is in Christ Jesus our Lord." (Romans 8:38-39)

Inspirational Insight:

Context: Paul speaks about the unbreakable bond of God's love for us. This verse reassures us of the unwavering and inseparable nature of God's love. It ties back to the poem by illustrating that no matter what we face, God's hand holds us firmly, and His love never falters.

Walking Together in Faith

"With every step, in faith I stand,
Knowing always, You hold my hand,
Through life's journey, near or far,
My guiding light, my morning star."

Bible Verse:

"The Lord makes firm the steps of the one who delights in him; though he may stumble, he will not fall, for the Lord upholds him with his hand." (Psalm 37:23-24)

Inspirational Insight:

Context: The psalmist speaks of God's faithfulness in guiding and supporting those who trust in Him. This verse highlights God's role in directing our steps and supporting us. It aligns with the poem by emphasizing that as we walk in faith, God's hand steadies and guides us, ensuring we do not fall.

My Walk With Him

Questions for Personal Reflection or Group Discussion

- How have you experienced God's hand guiding or comforting you in difficult times?
- In what areas of your life do you need to trust more in God's guidance and support?
- How does knowing that God holds your hand influence your daily walk of faith?

Guided Prayer

- "Dear Lord, thank You for holding my hand through every season of life. Help me to trust in Your guidance and strength, especially when I feel weak or uncertain. Remind me of Your constant presence and unfailing love. May I walk in faith, knowing that You are always by my side. Amen."

Fourteen

I am Weary, but With You I Can Prevail

Hey there! Welcome to another chapter of our journey of faith and discovery. In this chapter, we'll explore the concept of weariness and how, with God's strength, we can overcome and prevail. Through poetry, scripture, and uplifting insights, we'll see how He gives us the power to persevere through life's challenges.

I am Weary, but With You I Can Prevail

When burdens weigh heavy and strength runs low,
   When the path seems long, and my steps are slow,
   I lift my eyes to the hills divine,
   Knowing with You, I'll cross the finish line.

In moments of doubt, when fears assail,

My Walk With Him

When trials and troubles tip the scale,
Your voice whispers gently, "Child, you're mine,"
With You by my side, I know I'll be fine.

Through valleys deep and mountains high,
   When weariness threatens and hope runs dry,
   You refresh my soul with love sublime,
   Reminding me always, with You I'll shine.

When the world's chaos leaves me weak,
   And solace and peace I desperately seek,
   You offer rest, a gift so kind,
   In Your presence, strength I find.

So I'll press on, through thick and thin,
   Your grace empowering me from within,
   In every step, in every mile,
   With You, I know I can prevail.

Reflection

In this chapter, we're reminded that even in our weariness, God provides the strength we need to prevail. Recognizing our dependence on Him encourages us to lean on His power, find rest in His presence, and persevere through life's challenges. This chapter inspires us to keep moving forward, knowing that with God, we can overcome any obstacle.

When We Look, What We Find

Acknowledging Our Weariness
"When burdens weigh heavy and strength runs low,

I am Weary, but With You I Can Prevail

When the path seems long, and my steps are slow,
I lift my eyes to the hills divine,
Knowing with You, I'll cross the finish line."

Bible Verse:
"I lift up my eyes to the mountains—where does my help come from? My help comes from the Lord, the Maker of heaven and earth." (Psalm 121:1-2)

Inspirational Insight:
Context: Psalm 121 is a song of ascents, traditionally sung by pilgrims as they journeyed to Jerusalem. This verse reminds us to look to God as our source of help and strength when we feel weary. It ties back to the poem by emphasizing that even in our exhaustion, we can find the strength to continue our journey with God's help.

Finding Comfort in God's Presence
"In moments of doubt, when fears assail,
When trials and troubles tip the scale,
Your voice whispers gently, "Child, you're mine,"
With You by my side, I know I'll be fine."

Bible Verse:
"So do not fear, for I am with you; do not be dismayed, for I am your God. I will strengthen you and help you; I will uphold you with my righteous right hand." (Isaiah 41:10)

Inspirational Insight:
Context: Isaiah 41 contains God's words of comfort to Israel. This verse reassures us of God's constant presence and support,

especially in challenging times. It aligns with the poem by highlighting how God's presence gives us the confidence to face our fears and overcome our trials.

Renewed Strength in God's Love
"Through valleys deep and mountains high,
When weariness threatens and hope runs dry,
You refresh my soul with love sublime,
Reminding me always, with You I'll shine."

Bible Verse:
"But those who hope in the Lord will renew their strength. They will soar on wings like eagles; they will run and not grow weary, they will walk and not be faint." (Isaiah 40:31)

Inspirational Insight:
Context: Isaiah 40 speaks of God's comfort to His people. This verse highlights the renewal and strength that come from trusting in God. It resonates with the poem by reminding us that even in our weariness, God's love refreshes us and enables us to persevere.

Finding Peace in God's Presence
"When the world's chaos leaves me weak,
And solace and peace I desperately seek,
You offer rest, a gift so kind,
In Your presence, strength I find."

Bible Verse:
"Peace I leave with you; my peace I give you. I do not give to you as the world gives. Do not let your hearts be troubled and

I am Weary, but With You I Can Prevail

do not be afraid." (John 14:27)

Inspirational Insight:

Context: In John 14, Jesus prepares His disciples for His departure. He promises them a peace that surpasses worldly understanding. This verse reminds us that despite chaos and weakness, God offers us His peace as a gift. It's not a temporary or superficial peace but a deep, lasting peace from His presence. When we seek solace in God, we find rest and renewed strength. This peace is a buffer against the world's troubles, allowing us to find stability and courage in God's unchanging nature, even when everything around us seems unstable.

Prevailing Through God's Power

"So I'll press on, through thick and thin,
Your grace empowering me from within,
In every step, in every mile,
With You, I know I can prevail."

Bible Verse:

"I can do all this through him who gives me strength." (Philippians 4:13)

Inspirational Insight:

Context: In Philippians 4, Paul speaks about finding contentment in all circumstances. This verse emphasizes that we can overcome any challenge with God's strength. It aligns with the poem's conclusion, affirming that we can prevail in all situations through God's power.

Questions for Discussion

My Walk With Him

- Can you recall a time when you felt weary but found strength in God? How did this experience change your perspective?
- The poem mentions "lifting eyes to the hills divine." What practical ways you can shift your focus to God when feeling overwhelmed?
- How does knowing that God is always with you impact your ability to face challenges?

Guided Prayer

- Dear Heavenly Father, We come to You today, acknowledging our weariness and our need for Your strength. Thank You for Your unfailing love and constant presence in our lives. Lord, when our burdens feel heavy and our path seems long, help us to lift our eyes to You. Remind us that our help comes from You, the Maker of Heaven and Earth.
- In moments of doubt and fear, whisper Your comforting words to our hearts. Help us to feel Your presence beside us, giving us the confidence to face whatever lies ahead. Father, refresh our souls with Your love when our hope runs dry and weariness threatens to overwhelm us. Renew our strength as we put our trust in You. Please help us soar on wings like eagles, run and not grow weary, walk, and not faint.
- As we face life's challenges, keep our hearts and minds focused on You. May we always remember that You are our source of strength and hope even in our weariness.

Fifteen

Mercy is His Love, Undeserved

Hello again! In this chapter, we'll explore how God's mercy is a profound expression of His love, even when we feel undeserving. Through heartfelt poetry, meaningful scripture, and uplifting insights, we'll see how His mercy transforms our lives. Let's walk this path together and find hope and strength in His grace.

Mercy is His Love, Undeserved

In the depths of my heart, where shame often lies,
   I seek Your mercy, Lord, through tear-filled eyes.
   Though I falter and stray, unworthy of grace,
   Let me feel Your embrace, Your love in this place.

When the weight of my sins feels too much to bear,
   And I question Your love, wondering if You care,

Instead of wallowing in guilt and despair,
Mercy is Your love, undeserved yet rare.

In moments of doubt, when I feel so alone,
Help me remember the love I've been shown.
For every mistake, every wrong that I've done,
Let me find solace in the grace of Your Son.

Your mercy is a river, flowing endlessly free,
In the face of my failures, You still welcome me.
Through trials and heartache, Your promise remains,
Mercy is Your love, washing away all my stains.

Help me to share this mercy with those I encounter,
To offer compassion, to let love surmount.
In every interaction, let kindness abound,
For mercy is love, where true healing is found.

Reflection

This chapter explores how God's mercy reflects His love for us, even when we feel undeserving. From recognizing our need for grace to finding peace in His forgiveness, we learn that His mercy can transform our hearts. By extending mercy to others, we can be vessels of His love, turning our lives into testimonies of His grace.

This chapter encourages us to trust in God's unfailing love, find comfort in His mercy, and draw strength from His grace. Let's continue this faith journey, knowing His mercy is a constant source of hope and renewal.

Mercy is His Love, Undeserved

When We Look, What We Find

Seeing Mercy in Our Lives
 "In the depths of my heart, where shame often lies,
 I seek Your mercy, Lord, through tear-filled eyes.
 Though I falter and stray, unworthy of grace,
 Let me feel Your embrace, Your love in this place."

Bible Verse:
 "The Lord is gracious and compassionate, slow to anger and rich in love." (Psalm 145:8)

Inspirational Insight:
 Context: Psalm 145:8 reminds us of God's gracious and compassionate nature. This verse encourages us to see His mercy as a constant in our lives, assuring us that He is always ready to forgive and embrace us. It ties back to the poem by highlighting that even in our unworthiness, His love remains steadfast.

Finding Peace in Forgiveness
 "When the weight of my sins feels too much to bear,
 And I question Your love, wondering if You care,
 Instead of wallowing in guilt and despair,
 Mercy is Your love, undeserved yet rare."

Bible Verse:
 "If we confess our sins, he is faithful and just and will forgive us our sins and purify us from all unrighteousness." (1 John 1:9)

Inspirational Insight:
   Context: 1 John 1:9 assures us of forgiveness when we come to God with a repentant heart. This verse reminds us that His mercy cleanses us, allowing us to find peace in His forgiveness. It aligns with the poem by showing that we need not linger in guilt but can embrace His mercy.

Strength in Our Weakness
   "In moments of doubt, when I feel so alone,
   Help me remember the love I've been shown.
   For every mistake, every wrong that I've done,
   Let me find solace in the grace of Your Son."

Bible Verse:
   "My grace is sufficient for you, for my power is made perfect in weakness." (2 Corinthians 12:9)

Inspirational Insight:
   Context: 2 Corinthians 12:9 emphasizes that God's grace is enough for us, especially in our weaknesses. This verse reassures us that His power shines brightest when we acknowledge our need for Him. It connects to the poem by reminding us that our shortcomings can lead us closer to His grace.

Extending Mercy to Others
   "Help me to share this mercy with those I encounter,
   To offer compassion, to let love surmount.
   In every interaction, let kindness abound,
   For mercy is love, where true healing is found."

Bible Verse:

Mercy is His Love, Undeserved

"Be kind and compassionate to one another, forgiving each other, just as in Christ God forgave you." (Ephesians 4:32)

Inspirational Insight:
Context: Ephesians 4:32 calls us to reflect God's compassion in our relationships. This verse encourages us to extend mercy to others as we have received it. It ties back to the poem by showing that our experiences of mercy can inspire us to be conduits of His love.

A Testament to His Love
"For mercy is a river, flowing endlessly free,
In the face of my failures, You still welcome me.
Through trials and heartache, Your promise remains,
Mercy is Your love, washing away all my stains."

Bible Verse:
"For it is by grace you have been saved, through faith—and this is not from yourselves, it is the gift of God." (Ephesians 2:8)

Inspirational Insight:
Context: Ephesians 2:8 highlights the transformative power of God's grace. This verse reminds us that our salvation is a gift, a testament to His love. It connects with the poem by emphasizing that His mercy is a continual source of hope and renewal in our lives.

Questions for Personal Reflection or Group Discussion

My Walk With Him

- How have you experienced God's mercy in your life?
- In what ways can you extend mercy to others?
- What lessons have you learned about grace and forgiveness?

Guided Prayer

- "Dear Lord, thank You for Your new mercy every morning. Help me to recognize my need for Your grace and to extend that same mercy to others. Guide me to live in the light of Your love and to share it freely. Amen."

Sixteen

Whatever Happens, Rejoice in the Lord

Hello again! This chapter will explore the importance of rejoicing in the Lord, regardless of our circumstances. We'll discover how joy can be a powerful anchor in our lives through heartfelt poetry, meaningful scripture, and uplifting insights. Let's walk this path together and find hope and strength in His presence.

Whatever Happens, Rejoice in the Lord

In the highs and the lows, in the joy and the pain,
   Let my heart find its song, let my spirit remain.
   Though the storms may surround me, and trials may rise,
   Whatever happens, Lord, I'll lift up my eyes.

When the days feel heavy, and burdens weigh down,

Help me remember the joy that's always around.
Instead of dwelling on worries and fears,
Whatever happens, Lord, let me sing through the tears.

In moments of doubt, when my faith starts to wane,
Remind me, dear Lord, that You're with me in pain.
For every challenge I face, let me find grace,
Whatever happens, Lord, I'll seek Your embrace.

Your joy is my strength, a light in the dark,
It carries me through when my spirit feels stark.
Through every trial and heartache, Your love will sustain,
Whatever happens, Lord, I'll rejoice once again.

Help me to share this joy with those who are low,
To lift up the weary, to let Your love flow.
In every encounter, may kindness abound,
Whatever happens, Lord, let joy be my sound.

Reflection

In this chapter, we explore how rejoicing in the Lord can transform our perspective, even in challenging times. From finding joy amidst pain to sharing that joy with others, we learn that our faith can be a source of strength. By focusing on His goodness, we can celebrate His presence in our lives.

This chapter encourages us to trust in God's faithfulness, find comfort in His joy, and draw strength from His love. Let's continue this journey of faith, knowing that whatever happens, we can rejoice in the Lord.

Whatever Happens, Rejoice in the Lord

When We Look, What We Find

Finding Joy in Every Circumstance
 "In the highs and the lows, in the joy and the pain,
 Let my heart find its song, let my spirit remain.
 Though the storms may surround me, and trials may rise,
 Whatever happens, Lord, I'll lift up my eyes."

Bible Verse:
 "Rejoice in the Lord always. I will say it again: Rejoice!" (Philippians 4:4)
 Inspirational Insight:

Context: Philippians 4:4 is a powerful reminder to maintain a spirit of joy in all circumstances. This verse encourages us to rejoice in good times and always, knowing that our joy comes from the Lord. It ties back to the poem by emphasizing that our focus should be on Him, regardless of our situation.

Joy in the Midst of Trials
 "When the days feel heavy, and burdens weigh down,
 Help me remember the joy that's always around.
 Instead of dwelling on worries and fears,
 Whatever happens, Lord, let me sing through the tears."

Bible Verse:
 "Consider it pure joy, my brothers and sisters, whenever you face trials of many kinds." (James 1:2)
 Inspirational Insight:

Context: James 1:2 invites believers to find joy even in trials, recognizing that they produce growth and perseverance. This verse encourages us to shift our perspective, seeing challenges as opportunities for deeper faith. It connects with the poem by reminding us that joy can coexist with our struggles.

Strength in His Presence
"In moments of doubt, when my faith starts to wane,
Remind me, dear Lord, that You're with me in pain.
For every challenge I face, let me find grace,
Whatever happens, Lord, I'll seek Your embrace."

Bible Verse:
"The Lord is near to the brokenhearted and saves the crushed in spirit." (Psalm 34:18)
Inspirational Insight:

Context: Psalm 34:18 reassures us that God is close to us in our pain. This verse highlights His presence as a source of comfort and strength. It ties back to the poem by reminding us that we can find joy in knowing He is with us in our darkest moments.

Joy as Our Strength
"Your joy is my strength, a light in the dark,
It carries me through when my spirit feels stark.
Through every trial and heartache, Your love will sustain,
Whatever happens, Lord, I'll rejoice once again."

Bible Verse:
"The joy of the Lord is your strength." (Nehemiah 8:10)

Inspirational Insight:

Whatever Happens, Rejoice in the Lord

Context: Nehemiah 8:10 emphasizes that joy in the Lord empowers us to face challenges. This verse reminds us that true strength comes from our relationship with Him. It connects with the poem by affirming that His joy uplifts us, even in difficult times.

Sharing Joy with Others
"Help me to share this joy with those who are low,
To lift up the weary, to let Your love flow.
In every encounter, may kindness abound,
Whatever happens, Lord, let joy be my sound."

Bible Verse:
"Encourage one another and build each other up." (1 Thessalonians 5:11)

Inspirational Insight:
Context: 1 Thessalonians 5:11 calls us to support and uplift one another. This verse encourages us to share the joy we have in the Lord with others, fostering a community of encouragement. It ties back to the poem by showing that our joy can inspire and uplift those around us.

Questions for Personal Reflection or Group Discussion

- How have you experienced joy in difficult circumstances?
- What practices help you maintain a spirit of rejoicing?
- In what ways can you encourage others to find joy in the Lord?

My Walk With Him

Guided Prayer

- "Dear Lord, thank You for the joy that comes from knowing You. Help me to rejoice in all circumstances and to share that joy with others. May Your presence be my strength, and may I always lift my eyes to You. Amen."

Seventeen

What Do I Have That He Has Not Given

Welcome! In this chapter, we'll explore the profound truth that everything we possess is a gift from God. Through heartfelt poetry, meaningful scripture, and uplifting insights, we'll reflect on our blessings and the importance of gratitude. Let's walk this path together and find hope and strength in His provision.

What Do I Have That He Has Not Given?

In the quiet of my heart, when I pause to reflect,
   I ponder the blessings, the gifts I can't neglect.
   For every breath I take, for every moment I live,
   What do I have that He has not given?

When the world feels heavy, and I start to compare,

My Walk With Him

Help me remember the love that's always there.
Instead of longing for what others possess,
What do I have that He has not blessed?

In moments of doubt, when I question my worth,
Remind me, dear Lord, of my value since birth.
For every talent and gift, every joy I embrace,
What do I have that He has not placed?

Your grace is my anchor, Your love is my guide,
In the journey of life, You walk by my side.
Through trials and triumphs, Your blessings abound,
What do I have that You have not found?

Help me to share the gifts I've received,
To touch the lives of others, to help them believe.
In every encounter, let kindness be shown,
What do I have that He has not grown?

Reflection

In this chapter, we explore the idea that all we have is a gift from God. From recognizing our blessings to understanding our worth, we learn that gratitude opens our hearts to His abundance. By acknowledging His provision, we can cultivate a spirit of generosity and joy.

This chapter encourages us to trust in God's goodness, find comfort in His gifts, and draw strength from His love. Let's continue this faith journey, knowing that everything we have comes from Him.

What Do I Have That He Has Not Given

When We Look, What We Find

Recognizing Our Gifts
"In the quiet of my heart, when I pause to reflect,
I ponder the blessings, the gifts I can't neglect.
For every breath I take, for every moment I live,
What do I have that He has not given?"

Bible Verse:
"Every good and perfect gift is from above, coming down from the Father of the heavenly lights." (James 1:17)

Inspirational Insight:
Context: James 1:17 reminds us that all good things come from God. This verse encourages us to recognize that our blessings are not of our own making but are gifts from our loving Father. It ties back to the poem by emphasizing that everything we have results from His generosity.

Finding Contentment in His Provision
"When the world feels heavy, and I start to compare,
Help me remember the love that's always there.
Instead of longing for what others possess,
What do I have that He has not blessed?"

Bible Verse:
"But godliness with contentment is great gain." (1 Timothy 6:6)

Inspirational Insight:
Context: 1 Timothy 6:6 teaches us that true wealth comes

from being content with what we have. This verse encourages us to focus on our blessings rather than comparing ourselves to others. It connects with the poem by reminding us that our worth is found in His gifts, not in material possessions.

Understanding Our Worth
"In moments of doubt, when I question my worth,
Remind me, dear Lord, of my value since birth.
For every talent and gift, every joy I embrace,
What do I have that He has not placed?"

Bible Verse:
"I praise you because I am fearfully and wonderfully made." (Psalm 139:14)

Inspirational Insight:
Context: Psalm 139:14 affirms our intrinsic value as God's creations. This verse reassures us that we are uniquely designed and loved. It ties back to the poem by highlighting that our worth comes from being made in His image, filled with His gifts.

Embracing His Grace
"Your grace is my anchor, Your love is my guide,
In the journey of life, You walk by my side.
Through trials and triumphs, Your blessings abound,
What do I have that You have not found?"

Bible Verse:
"My grace is sufficient for you, for my power is made perfect in weakness." (2 Corinthians 12:9)

What Do I Have That He Has Not Given

Inspirational Insight:

Context: 2 Corinthians 12:9 emphasizes that God's grace is enough for us. This verse reassures us that His power shines through our weaknesses. It connects with the poem by reminding us that His grace is a gift that sustains us in every season of life.

Sharing Our Blessings

"Help me to share the gifts I've received,
To touch the lives of others, to help them believe.
In every encounter, let kindness be shown,
What do I have that He has not grown?"

Bible Verse:

"Freely you have received; freely give." (Matthew 10:8)

Inspirational Insight:

Context: Matthew 10:8 calls us to share the blessings we've received. This verse encourages us to be generous and to use our gifts to help others. It ties back to the poem by showing that our abundance is meant to be shared, reflecting His love in the world.

Questions for Personal Reflection or Group Discussion

- What blessings can you recognize in your life that are gifts from God?
- How can you cultivate contentment with what you have?
- In what ways can you share your gifts with others?

My Walk With Him

Guided Prayer

- "Dear Lord, thank You for the gifts You have given me. Help me to recognize Your blessings in my life and to share them with others. May I find contentment in Your provision and always remember that everything I have comes from You. Amen."

Eighteen

Please Don't Judge as I Deserve

Hello again! In this chapter, we'll explore the theme of grace and understanding, recognizing that we all fall short and need compassion. Through heartfelt poetry, meaningful scripture, and uplifting insights, we'll reflect on the importance of mercy in our relationships with others and ourselves. Let's walk this path together and find hope and strength in His grace.

Please Don't Judge as I Deserve

In the shadows of my heart, where guilt often hides,
   I plead for Your mercy, where true love abides.
   Though I stumble and fall, unworthy of grace,
   Please don't judge as I deserve; let me seek Your face.

When the weight of my sins feels too much to bear,
   Help me remember the love that's always there.

Instead of condemnation for the wrongs I've done,
   Please don't judge as I deserve; let Your grace be my sun.

In moments of shame, when I feel so alone,
   Remind me, dear Lord, of the love I have known.
   For every failure I face, every tear that I cry,
   Please don't judge as I deserve; let mercy draw nigh.

Your kindness is my refuge, Your love my embrace,
   In the depths of my struggle, I seek Your grace.
   Through trials and heartache, Your compassion I find,
   Please don't judge as I deserve; let Your heart be my guide.

Help me to share this mercy with those who are lost,
   To offer understanding, no matter the cost.
   In every encounter, let kindness abound,
   Please don't judge as I deserve; let love be profound.

Reflection

In this chapter, we explore the power of grace and the importance of not judging others or ourselves harshly. From recognizing our need for mercy to extending that same grace to others, we learn that compassion can heal and restore. By embracing His love, we can create a community built on understanding and forgiveness.

This chapter encourages us to trust in God's infinite mercy, find comfort in His grace, and draw strength from His love. Let's continue this faith journey, knowing that we all deserve compassion.

Please Don't Judge as I Deserve

When We Look, What We Find

Seeking Mercy in Our Lives
"In the shadows of my heart, where guilt often hides,
I plead for Your mercy, where true love abides.
Though I stumble and fall, unworthy of grace,
Please don't judge as I deserve; let me seek Your face."

Bible Verse:
"For all have sinned and fall short of the glory of God." (Romans 3:23)

Inspirational Insight:
Context: Romans 3:23 reminds us that we all fall short and need God's grace. This verse encourages us to approach others humbly, recognizing our shared humanity. It ties back to the poem by emphasizing that none of us are beyond the need for mercy.

Finding Comfort in His Love
"When the weight of my sins feels too much to bear,
Help me remember the love that's always there.
Instead of condemnation for the wrongs I've done,
Please don't judge as I deserve; let Your grace be my sun."

Bible Verse:
"There is now no condemnation for those who are in Christ Jesus." (Romans 8:1)

Inspirational Insight:
Context: Romans 8:1 assures us that we are free from

condemnation in Christ. This verse encourages us to embrace His forgiveness and to let go of guilt. It connects with the poem by reminding us that His grace shines brightly, illuminating our path.

Healing Through Understanding
"In moments of shame, when I feel so alone,
Remind me, dear Lord, of the love I have known.
For every failure I face, every tear that I cry,
Please don't judge as I deserve; let mercy draw nigh."

Bible Verse:
"The Lord is close to the brokenhearted and saves those who are crushed in spirit." (Psalm 34:18)

Inspirational Insight:
Context: Psalm 34:18 highlights God's compassion for the brokenhearted. This verse reassures us that He is near in our pain. It ties back to the poem by emphasizing that His mercy is a source of healing and comfort in our struggles.

Guided by His Compassion
"Your kindness is my refuge, Your love my embrace,
In the depths of my struggle, I seek Your grace.
Through trials and heartache, Your compassion I find,
Please don't judge as I deserve; let Your heart be my guide."
Bible Verse:

"But God, being rich in mercy, because of the great love with which he loved us." (Ephesians 2:4)

Please Don't Judge as I Deserve

Inspirational Insight:

Context: Ephesians 2:4 reminds us of God's abundant mercy and love. This verse encourages us to lean on His compassion during difficult times. It connects with the poem by affirming His heart is always open to us, guiding us through our trials.

Sharing Mercy with Others

"Help me to share this mercy with those who are lost,
To offer understanding, no matter the cost.
In every encounter, let kindness abound,
Please don't judge as I deserve; let love be profound."

Bible Verse:

"Be kind and compassionate to one another, forgiving each other, just as in Christ God forgave you." (Ephesians 4:32)

Inspirational Insight:

Context: Ephesians 4:32 calls us to practice kindness and forgiveness. This verse encourages us to extend the grace we have received to others. It ties back to the poem by showing that our experiences of mercy should inspire us to love and understand those around us.

Questions for Personal Reflection or Group Discussion

- How have you experienced God's mercy in your life?
- In what ways can you practice kindness and understanding towards others?
- How can you learn to forgive yourself as God forgives you?

My Walk With Him

Guided Prayer

- "Dear Lord, thank You for Your mercy and grace. Help me to remember that I am not defined by my failures but by Your love. Teach me to extend that same grace to others and approach every situation compassionately. May I always seek Your face and find comfort in Your embrace. Amen."

Nineteen

He Died is My Why

Hello again! In this chapter, we'll delve into the profound truth of Christ's sacrifice and how it shapes our purpose and identity. Through heartfelt poetry, meaningful scripture, and uplifting insights, we'll reflect on the significance of His death and resurrection in our lives. Let's walk this path together and find hope and strength in His love.

He Died Is My Why

In the stillness of my heart, when doubts start to rise,
   I remember the Savior, who paid the ultimate price.
   For every sin I carry, for every tear I cry,
   He died is my why; His love is my tie.

When the weight of the world feels heavy and cold,
   Help me remember the story of love that's been told.

My Walk With Him

Instead of despairing when trials come nigh,
He died is my why; His grace lifts me high.

In moments of struggle, when I feel so alone,
   Remind me, dear Lord, that I'm never on my own.
   For every burden I bear, every fear I defy,
   He died is my why; His hope is my sky.

Your sacrifice frees me, Your love sets me free,
   In the depths of my sorrow, You're always with me.
   Through shadows and darkness, Your light will not die,
   He died is my why; His truth is my cry.

Help me to share this message with those who are lost,
   To show them the love that came at such a cost.
   In every encounter, may Your love multiply,
   He died is my why; His grace is my why.

Reflection

In this chapter, we explore the significance of Christ's sacrifice and how it informs our purpose. From recognizing His love to sharing that message with others, we learn that His death is the foundation of our faith. By embracing His truth, we can live with purpose and joy.

This chapter encourages us to trust in the power of His sacrifice, find comfort in His love, and draw strength from His resurrection. Let's continue this journey of faith, knowing that His death is the reason we have hope.

He Died is My Why

When We Look, What We Find

Understanding Our Purpose
"In the stillness of my heart, when doubts start to rise,
I remember the Savior, who paid the ultimate price.
For every sin I carry, for every tear I cry,
He died is my why; His love is my tie."

Bible Verse:
"For God so loved the world that he gave his one and only Son." (John 3:16)

Inspirational Insight:
Context: John 3:16 highlights the depth of God's love through the sacrifice of His Son. This verse reminds us that His death was a gift for our salvation. It ties back to the poem by emphasizing that His love is the foundation of our faith.

Finding Strength in His Sacrifice
"When the weight of the world feels heavy and cold,
Help me remember the story of love that's been told.
Instead of despairing when trials come nigh,
He died is my why; His grace lifts me high."

Bible Verse:
"By his wounds, we are healed." (Isaiah 53:5)

Inspirational Insight:
Context: Isaiah 53:5 speaks to the healing power of Christ's sacrifice. This verse encourages us to find strength in His suffering. It connects with the poem by reminding us that His

grace empowers us through our struggles.

Hope in Our Struggles
"In moments of struggle, when I feel so alone,
Remind me, dear Lord, that I'm never on my own.
For every burden I bear, every fear I defy,
He died is my why; His hope is my sky."

Bible Verse:
"Cast all your anxiety on him because he cares for you." (1 Peter 5:7)

Inspirational Insight:
Context: 1 Peter 5:7 encourages us to bring our worries to God. This verse reassures us that He cares deeply for us. It ties back to the poem by emphasizing that His love provides comfort in our darkest moments.

Light in the Darkness
"Your sacrifice frees me, Your love sets me free,
In the depths of my sorrow, You're always with me.
Through shadows and darkness, Your light will not die,
He died is my why; His truth is my cry."

Bible Verse:
"I am the light of the world. Whoever follows me will never walk in darkness." (John 8:12)

Inspirational Insight:
Context: John 8:12 assures us that Christ is our guiding light. This verse encourages us to walk in His truth, knowing that

He Died is My Why

He dispels darkness. It connects with the poem by reminding us that His presence illuminates our path.

Sharing His Love
  "Help me to share this message with those who are lost,
  To show them the love that came at such a cost.
  In every encounter, may Your love multiply,
  He died is my why; His grace is my why."

Bible Verse:
  "Go therefore and make disciples of all nations." (Matthew 28:19)

Inspirational Insight:
  Context: Matthew 28:19 calls us to share the gospel with others. This verse encourages us to spread His love and truth. It ties back to the poem by emphasizing that our purpose is to reflect His grace to the world.

Questions for Personal Reflection or Group Discussion

- How does Christ's sacrifice shape your understanding of love and purpose?
- In what ways can you share the message of His love with others?
- How can you find strength in His sacrifice during difficult times?

Guided Prayer

My Walk With Him

"Dear Lord, thank You for the sacrifice of Your Son. Help me to remember that His death is the foundation of my faith and purpose. Teach me to walk in His light and share His love with those around me. May I always find hope in the truth that He died is my why. Amen.

Twenty

When All Fades Away, He Remains

Hello again! In this chapter, we'll explore the enduring nature of God's presence and love, especially in times of uncertainty and change. Through heartfelt poetry, meaningful scripture, and uplifting insights, we'll reflect on the assurance that He remains steadfast even when everything else fades. Let's walk this path together and find hope and strength in His eternal nature.

When All Fades Away, He Remains

In the chaos of life, when storms start to rise,
   I find my foundation, where true comfort lies.
   When the world feels uncertain, and shadows draw near,
   When all fades away, He remains; I have no fear.

As the seasons are changing, and moments slip by,

My Walk With Him

Help me remember the truth that won't die.
For every fleeting moment, every tear that I shed,
When all fades away, He remains; my spirit is fed.

In the depths of my sorrow, when hope seems so far,
   Remind me, dear Lord, that You're never afar.
   For every heartache I face, every doubt that I claim,
   When all fades away, He remains; forever the same.

Your love is my anchor, Your grace is my song,
   In the midst of the trials, You help me stay strong.
   Through the ebb and the flow, through joy and through pain,
   When all fades away, He remains; my heart will sustain.

Help me to trust in the promise You give,
   To find peace in Your presence, in the way that I live.
   In every moment of doubt, may my faith not wane,
   When all fades away, He remains; my hope will not wane.

Reflection

In this chapter, we explore God's unwavering presence in our lives. From recognizing His constancy to finding comfort in His love, we learn that He is our eternal refuge. We can face life's uncertainties with confidence and peace by embracing His truth.

This chapter encourages us to trust in His enduring nature, find solace in His love, and draw strength from His promises. Let's continue this faith journey, knowing that He remains when all else fades.

When All Fades Away, He Remains

When We Look, What We Find

Finding Our Foundation
 "In the chaos of life, when storms start to rise,
 I find my foundation, where true comfort lies.
 When the world feels uncertain, and shadows draw near,
 When all fades away, He remains; I have no fear."

Bible Verse:
 "Jesus Christ is the same yesterday and today and forever." (Hebrews 13:8)

Inspirational Insight:
 Context: Hebrews 13:8 assures us of Christ's unchanging nature. This verse reminds us that no matter the circumstances, He is always faithful. It ties back to the poem by emphasizing that we can find security in His constancy.

Strength in Change
 "As the seasons are changing, and moments slip by,
 Help me remember the truth that won't die.
 For every fleeting moment, every tear that I shed,
 When all fades away, He remains; my spirit is fed."

Bible Verse:
 "Heaven and earth will pass away, but my words will never pass away." (Matthew 24:35)

Inspirational Insight:
 Context: Matthew 24:35 highlights the permanence of God's word. This verse encourages us to cling to His promises,

knowing they endure. It connects with the poem by reminding us that His truth sustains us through life's changes.

Hope in Sorrow
"In the depths of my sorrow, when hope seems so far,
Remind me, dear Lord, that You're never afar.
For every heartache I face, every doubt that I claim,
When all fades away, He remains; forever the same."

Bible Verse:
"The Lord is close to the brokenhearted and saves those who are crushed in spirit." (Psalm 34:18)

Inspirational Insight:
Context: Psalm 34:18 reassures us of God's nearness in our pain. This verse reminds us that He is always with us, providing comfort. It ties back to the poem by emphasizing that His presence brings healing in our sorrow.

Anchored in His Love
"Your love is my anchor, Your grace is my song,
In the midst of the trials, You help me stay strong.
Through the ebb and the flow, through joy and through pain,
When all fades away, He remains; my heart will sustain."

Bible Verse:
"Cast all your anxiety on him because he cares for you." (1 Peter 5:7)

Inspirational Insight:
Context: 1 Peter 5:7 encourages us to bring our worries to

When All Fades Away, He Remains

God. This verse reassures us of His caring nature. It connects with the poem by reminding us that His love supports us through every challenge.

Trusting His Promises
   "Help me to trust in the promise You give,
   To find peace in Your presence, in the way that I live.
   In every moment of doubt, may my faith not wane,
   When all fades away, He remains; my hope will not wane."

Bible Verse:
"For I know the plans I have for you," declares the Lord, "plans to prosper you and not to harm you, plans to give you hope and a future." (Jeremiah 29:11)

Inspirational Insight:
Context: Jeremiah 29:11 assures us of God's good plans for our lives. This verse encourages us to trust in His guidance, knowing He has our best interests at heart. It ties back to the poem by emphasizing that our hope is secure in Him.

Questions for Personal Reflection or Group Discussion

- How have you experienced God's presence during difficult times?
- In what ways can you remind yourself of His unchanging nature?
- How can you cultivate trust in God's promises in your daily life?

My Walk With Him

Guided Prayer

- "Dear Lord, thank You for being my constant in a changing world. Help me to remember that when all else fades, You remain. Teach me to trust in Your promises and find peace in Your presence. May I always seek Your love and strength in every moment? Amen."

Twenty-One

For Love and Grace

Once again, welcome to another chapter of our journey of faith and discovery. In this chapter, we'll explore the profound depths of love, its costs, and the grace that sustains us through life's challenges. Through poetry, scripture, and uplifting insights, we'll see how embracing joy and sorrow leads us to a deeper understanding of God's love and purpose for our lives.

A Prayer for Love and Grace

Oh Lord, I ponder love's profound cost,
   What's the point of joy when it leads to loss?
   If I say "yes" to the gift, then I'll embrace the pain,
   For every scar begins with a smile's sweet refrain.

Each cry of "why" echoes with a joy's bright start,
   A reminder that love is a dance of the heart.

My Walk With Him

Help me find the courage to care and to share,
For in every struggle, I know You are there.

You are my destination, my goal, my guiding light,
   In moments of darkness, You shine ever bright.
   Without the strife, where's the life to be found?
   For it is in trials and triumphs that Your grace does abound.

So let me not shy from the storms that may come,
   For through every challenge, I'll find that with You, I am strong.
   The goal is not to escape or to flee,
   But to rest in your love, to be truly free.

In every hardship I find, I'll seek your embrace,
   Finding solace in the grace that You place.
   For love, in its fullness, is worth every tear,
   In Your arms, dear Lord, I have nothing to fear.

So I'll journey onward, with faith as my guide,
   Embracing each moment, with You by my side.
   For in love's grand tapestry, woven with care,
   I find life's true purpose, Your sacrifice forever laid bare.

Reflection

This chapter reminds us of the profound nature of love and its inseparable connection to joy and sorrow. We explore the courage it takes to embrace life fully, knowing that every moment of happiness carries the potential for pain. By recognizing God as our ultimate destination and source of strength, we find the resilience to face life's challenges with grace and purpose.

This chapter inspires us to see the beauty in life's highs and lows, understanding that without struggles, we cannot fully appreciate the depth of God's love and the richness of our experiences. It encourages us to find solace in God's grace and presence, reminding us that the point of life is not to avoid trials but to grow through them with faith and unwavering trust in God's plan.

When We Look, What We Find

Embracing Love's Cost
   "Oh Lord, I ponder love's profound cost,
   What's the point of joy when it leads to loss?
   If I say "yes" to the gift, I embrace the pain,
   For every scar begins with a smile's sweet refrain."

Bible Verse:
   "I have told you these things, so that in me you may have peace. In this world you will have trouble. But take heart! I have overcome the world." (John 16:33)

Inspirational Insight:
   Context: Jesus prepares His disciples for the challenges they will face. This verse reminds us that while life brings joy and sorrow, we can find peace in Christ. It ties back to the poem by acknowledging that embracing love means accepting its joys and pains, knowing Christ has ultimately overcome all.

Finding Courage in God's Presence
"Each cry of "why" echoes with a joy's bright start,
A reminder that love is a dance of the heart.
Help me find the courage to care and to share,
For in every struggle, I know you are there."

Bible Verse:
"Be strong and courageous. Do not be afraid or terrified because of them, for the Lord your God goes with you; he will never leave you nor forsake you." (Deuteronomy 31:6)

Inspirational Insight:
Context: Moses encourages the Israelites as they prepare to enter the Promised Land. This verse assures us of God's constant presence, giving us the courage to face life's challenges. It aligns with the poem by reminding us that God is with us in every struggle, empowering us to love and share despite the risks.

God as Our Guiding Light
"You are my destination, my goal, my guiding light,
In moments of darkness, You shine ever bright.
Without the strife, where's the life to be found?
For it is in trials and triumphs that Your grace does abound."

Bible Verse:
"Your word is a lamp for my feet, a light on my path." (Psalm 119:105)

Inspirational Insight:
Context: The psalmist praises God's word as a guide for life.

For Love and Grace

This verse highlights God's role as our guide and light in all circumstances. It ties beautifully with the poem by affirming that God illuminates our path, helping us find meaning in both our trials and triumphs.

Finding Strength in Challenges
"So let me not shy from the storms that may come,
For through every challenge, I'll find that with You, I am strong.
The goal is not to escape or to flee,
But to rest in your love, to be truly free."

Bible Verse:
"I can do all this through him who gives me strength." (Philippians 4:13)

Inspirational Insight:
Context: Paul expresses his confidence in Christ's empowering presence. This verse reminds us that our strength comes from God, enabling us to face any challenge. It aligns with the poem by encouraging us to embrace life's storms, knowing that true freedom rests in God's love and strength.

Finding Solace in God's Grace
"So I'll journey onward, with faith as my guide,
Embracing each moment with You by my side.
For in love's grand tapestry, woven with care,
I find life's true purpose, Your sacrifice forever laid bare."

Bible Verse:
"But he said to me, 'My grace is sufficient for you, for my

power is made perfect in weakness.'" (2 Corinthians 12:9)

Inspirational Insight:

Context: God responds to Paul's prayer for relief from his "thorn in the flesh." This verse highlights the sufficiency of God's grace in all circumstances. It ties back to the poem by reminding us that God's grace provides solace and strength in every hardship, making love worth every tear shed.

Questions for Personal Reflection or Group Discussion

- How has experiencing joy and sorrow deepened your understanding of God's love?
- In what ways have you found God's presence as a guiding light in your darkest moments?
- How can you cultivate the courage to embrace life's challenges, knowing that God's grace is sufficient?

Guided Prayer

- "Dear Lord, thank You for the gift of love, with all its joys and sorrows. Help me find courage in Your presence to embrace life fully, seeing Your guiding light in both trials and triumphs. May I always rest in Your love, finding strength in Your grace and freedom in Your embrace. Guide me on this journey of faith, knowing that I find life's true purpose in You. Amen."

Twenty-Two

I Am But Clay in the Potter's Hands

Hello again! In this chapter, we'll explore the beautiful imagery of being shaped and molded by God, our Creator. We'll reflect on our identity as vessels in His hands through heartfelt poetry, meaningful scripture, and uplifting insights. Let's walk this path together and find hope and strength in His craftsmanship.

I Am but Clay in the Potter's Hands

In the quiet of my soul, where dreams start to form,
   I yield to the Potter, who shapes me in the storm.
   Though I may feel fragile, and my edges may fray,
   I am but clay in the Potter's hands; He guides my way.

When the world tries to break me, and doubts start to rise,
   Help me remember the truth that opens my eyes.
   For every crack and imperfection, every tear that I shed,

My Walk With Him

I am but clay in the Potter's hands; His love is my thread.

In the heat of the trials, when I feel so alone,
   Remind me, dear Lord, that I'm never on my own.
   For every struggle I face, every fear that I dread,
   I am but clay in the Potter's hands; my spirit is fed.

Your grace is my vessel, Your love is my mold,
   In the depths of Your wisdom, I find strength untold.
   Through the shaping and forming, through joy and through pain,
   I am but clay in the Potter's hands; my heart will remain.

Help me to trust in the process You lead,
   To embrace every moment, to follow Your creed.
   In every twist and turn, may my faith not wane,
   I am but clay in the Potter's hands; His purpose I gain.

Reflection

This chapter explores the transformative power of being shaped by God. From recognizing our need for His guidance to embracing the journey of becoming, we learn that we are His cherished creations. By yielding to His hands, we can discover our true identity.

This chapter encourages us to trust in the Potter's plan, find comfort in His love, and draw strength from His craftsmanship. Let's continue this faith journey, knowing that we are beautifully made in His image.

I Am But Clay in the Potter's Hands

When We Look, What We Find

Yielding to the Potter
"In the quiet of my soul, where dreams start to form,
I yield to the Potter, who shapes me in the storm.
Though I may feel fragile, and my edges may fray,
I am but clay in the Potter's hands; He guides my way."

Bible Verse:
"But now, O Lord, You are our Father; we are the clay, and You are our potter; and we are all the work of Your hand." (Isaiah 64:8)

Inspirational Insight:
Context: Isaiah 64:8 beautifully illustrates our relationship with God as the Creator. This verse reminds us that we are in His hands, shaped by His purpose. It ties back to the poem by emphasizing our identity as His creation.

Strength in Imperfection
"When the world tries to break me, and doubts start to rise,
Help me remember the truth that opens my eyes.
For every crack and imperfection, every tear that I shed,
I am but clay in the Potter's hands; His love is my thread."

Bible Verse:
"My grace is sufficient for you, for my power is made perfect in weakness." (2 Corinthians 12:9)

Inspirational Insight:
Context: 2 Corinthians 12:9 reassures us that God's grace

covers our weaknesses. This verse encourages us to embrace our imperfections, knowing they highlight His strength. It connects with the poem by reminding us that His love holds us together.

Hope in Trials
"In the heat of the trials, when I feel so alone,
Remind me, dear Lord, that I'm never on my own.
For every struggle I face, every fear that I dread,
I am but clay in the Potter's hands; my spirit is fed."

Bible Verse:
"Consider it pure joy, my brothers and sisters, whenever you face trials of many kinds." (James 1:2)

Inspirational Insight:
Context: James 1:2 encourages us to find joy in trials, knowing they refine our faith. This verse reminds us that challenges are part of our shaping process. It ties back to the poem by emphasizing that our spirit is nourished through adversity.

Embracing His Craftsmanship
"Your grace is my vessel, Your love is my mold,
In the depths of Your wisdom, I find strength untold.
Through the shaping and forming, through joy and through pain,
I am but clay in the Potter's hands; my heart will remain."

Bible Verse:
"For we are God's handiwork, created in Christ Jesus to do

I Am But Clay in the Potter's Hands

good works." (Ephesians 2:10)

Inspirational Insight:

Context: Ephesians 2:10 affirms our identity as God's masterpiece. This verse encourages us to embrace our purpose in Him. It connects with the poem by reminding us that we are crafted for good works.

Trusting the Process
"Help me to trust in the process You lead,
To embrace every moment, to follow Your creed.
In every twist and turn, may my faith not wane,
I am but clay in the Potter's hands; His purpose I gain."

Bible Verse:
"And we know that in all things God works for the good of those who love him." (Romans 8:28)

Inspirational Insight:

Context: Romans 8:28 reassures us that God is at work in our lives for our good. This verse encourages us to trust His plan, knowing He has our best interests in mind. It ties back to the poem by emphasizing that His purpose unfolds in our lives.

Questions for Personal Reflection or Group Discussion

- How do you see yourself as clay in the Potter's hands?
- In what ways can you embrace the process of being shaped by God?

- How can you find strength in your imperfections and trust in His craftsmanship?

Guided Prayer

- "Dear Lord, thank You for being the Potter in my life. Help me to yield to Your shaping hands and trust in the process You have for me. May I embrace every moment as a part of Your beautiful design. I am but clay in Your hands, and I trust in Your purpose. Amen."

Twenty-Three

But for the Grace of God, Go I

Hello again! In this chapter, we'll explore the transformative power of God's grace in our lives. Through heartfelt poetry, meaningful scripture, and uplifting insights, we'll reflect on how His grace sustains us and shapes our journey. Let's walk this path together and find hope and strength in His unmerited favor.

But for the Grace of God, Go I

In the shadows of my past, where mistakes often lie,
   I pause to remember the grace that draws nigh.
   For every stumble I've taken, every tear that I cry,
   His love lifts me high and but for His grace, go I;

When I see others struggling, lost in their pain,
   Help me to remember I'm to be part of the chain.

My Walk With Him

For every heart that is broken, every soul that's awry,
   His mercy is sufficient and but for His grace, go I.

In the moments of weakness, when I falter and fall,
   Remind me, dear Lord, that Your grace covers all.
   For every doubt that I harbor, every fear that I try,
   Your strength is my high and but for Your grace, go I.

Your love is my refuge, Your kindness my song,
   In the depths of my failures, You help me stay strong.
   Through the trials and heartaches, through joy and through sigh,
   My spirit will fly and but for Your Grace go I.

Help me to share this grace with those who feel lost,
   To show them Your love, no matter the cost.
   In every encounter, may compassion be my reply,
   Your love is my why and but for Your grace go I.

Reflection

In this chapter, we explore the profound impact of God's grace on our lives. From recognizing our need for His mercy to extending that grace to others, we learn that His unmerited favor is what sustains us. By embracing His grace, we can live with humility and joy.

This chapter encourages us to trust in the power of His grace, find comfort in His love, and draw strength from His forgiveness. Let's continue this journey of faith, knowing that it is by His grace we stand.

But for the Grace of God, Go I

When We Look, What We Find

Embracing His Grace
 "In the shadows of my past, where mistakes often lie,
 I pause to remember the grace that draws nigh.
 For every stumble I've taken, every tear that I cry,
 His love lifts me high and but for His grace, go I."

Bible Verse:
 "For it is by grace you have been saved, through faith—and this is not from yourselves, it is the gift of God." (Ephesians 2:8)

Inspirational Insight:
 Context: Ephesians 2:8 highlights the gift of grace as the foundation of our salvation. This verse reminds us that we cannot earn God's favor; it is freely given. It ties back to the poem by emphasizing that His love is what elevates us.

Compassion for Others
 "When I see others struggling, lost in their pain,
 Help me to remember I'm to be part of the chain.
 For every heart that is broken, every soul that's awry,
 His mercy is sufficient and but for His grace, go I."

Bible Verse:
 "Be kind and compassionate to one another, forgiving each other, just as in Christ God forgave you." (Ephesians 4:32)

Inspirational Insight:
 Context: Ephesians 4:32 encourages us to extend the same

grace we receive to others. This verse reminds us that our compassion is rooted in God's forgiveness. It connects with the poem by emphasizing our shared need for mercy.

Strength in Weakness
"In the moments of weakness, when I falter and fall,
Remind me, dear Lord, that Your grace covers all.
For every doubt that I harbor, every fear that I try,
Your strength is my high and but for Your grace, go I."

Bible Verse:
"My grace is sufficient for you, for my power is made perfect in weakness." (2 Corinthians 12:9)

Inspirational Insight:
Context: 2 Corinthians 12:9 reassures us that God's grace empowers us in our weaknesses. This verse encourages us to rely on His strength rather than our own. It ties back to the poem by reminding us that His grace sustains us.

Finding Refuge in His Love
"Your love is my refuge, Your kindness my song,
In the depths of my failures, You help me stay strong.
Through the trials and heartaches, through joy and through sigh,
My spirit will fly and but for Your Grace go I."

Bible Verse:
"The Lord is gracious and compassionate, slow to anger and rich in love." (Psalm 145:8)

But for the Grace of God, Go I

Inspirational Insight:

Context: Psalm 145:8 highlights the character of God as gracious and compassionate. This verse reassures us of His loving nature. It connects with the poem by emphasizing that His love is our source of strength.

Sharing His Grace

"Help me to share this grace with those who feel lost,
To show them Your love, no matter the cost.
In every encounter, may compassion be my reply,
Your love is my why and but for Your grace go I."

Bible Verse:
"Freely you have received; freely give." (Matthew 10:8)

Inspirational Insight:

Context: Matthew 10:8 encourages us to share the grace we have received. This verse reminds us that our blessings are meant to be shared with others. It ties back to the poem by emphasizing our call to extend His love.

Questions for Personal Reflection or Group Discussion

- How has God's grace impacted your life?
- In what ways can you extend grace to others in your daily interactions?
- How can you remind yourself of the importance of humility in light of His grace?

My Walk With Him

Guided Prayer

- "Dear Lord, thank You for the gift of Your grace in my life. Help me to recognize my need for Your mercy and to extend that same grace to others. May I always remember that but for Your grace, I would be lost. Guide my heart to reflect Your love. Amen."

Twenty-Four

As for Me, I Will Serve the Lord

Hello again! In this chapter, we'll explore the commitment to serve God wholeheartedly. Through heartfelt poetry, meaningful scripture, and uplifting insights, we'll reflect on what it means to dedicate our lives to His service. Let's walk this path together and find hope and strength in our calling.

As for Me, I Will Serve the Lord

In the quiet of my heart, where decisions are made,
   I choose to follow the path where Your love won't fade.
   Though the world may distract me, and doubts may take hold,
   As for me, I will serve the Lord; His truth is my gold.

When the trials surround me, and the road feels unclear,
   Help me remember the promise that casts out all fear.

For every challenge I face, every mountain I climb,
As for me, I will serve the Lord; His grace is my rhyme.

In the moments of weakness, when my strength starts to wane,
Remind me, dear Lord, that Your power sustains.
For every tear that I shed, every sigh that I breathe,
As for me, I will serve the Lord; in Him, I believe.

Your love is my compass, Your word is my guide,
In the depths of my journey, I'll walk by Your side.
Through the highs and the lows, through joy and through strife,
As for me, I will serve the Lord; He's the source of my life.

Help me to shine Your light in a world that feels dark,
To share Your love freely, to ignite every spark.
In every action I take, may my heart be aligned,
As for me, I will serve the Lord; His purpose I find.

Reflection

In this chapter, we explore the commitment to serve God with our whole hearts. From recognizing our calling to embracing the joy of service, we learn that our dedication transforms not only our lives but also those around us. By choosing to serve, we reflect His love and purpose.

This chapter encourages us to trust in His guidance, find strength in His promises, and live out our commitment to Him. Let's continue this journey of faith, knowing that our service is a response to His incredible grace.

As for Me, I Will Serve the Lord

When We Look, What We Find

Choosing to Serve
"In the quiet of my heart, where decisions are made,
I choose to follow the path where Your love won't fade.
Though the world may distract me, and doubts may take hold,
As for me, I will serve the Lord; His truth is my gold."

Bible Verse:
"But as for me and my household, we will serve the Lord." (Joshua 24:15)

Inspirational Insight:
Context: Joshua 24:15 emphasizes the importance of making a deliberate choice to serve God. This verse serves as a powerful reminder that our commitment shapes our lives. It ties back to the poem by affirming our decision to follow Him.

Facing Trials with Faith
"When the trials surround me, and the road feels unclear,
Help me remember the promise that casts out all fear.
For every challenge I face, every mountain I climb,
As for me, I will serve the Lord; His grace is my rhyme."

Bible Verse:
"I can do all this through Him who gives me strength." (Philippians 4:13)

Inspirational Insight:
Context: Philippians 4:13 reassures us that we can face any

challenge with Christ's strength. This verse encourages us to rely on His power in our service. It connects with the poem by reminding us that His grace empowers us.

Strength in Weakness
"In the moments of weakness, when my strength starts to wane,
Remind me, dear Lord, that Your power sustains.
For every tear that I shed, every sigh that I breathe,
As for me, I will serve the Lord; in Him, I believe."

Bible Verse:
"My grace is sufficient for you, for my power is made perfect in weakness." (2 Corinthians 12:9)

Inspirational Insight:
Context: 2 Corinthians 12:9 emphasizes that God's grace is sufficient in our weaknesses. This verse encourages us to embrace our reliance on Him. It ties back to the poem by underscoring our faith in His sustaining power.

Guidance in His Word
"Your love is my compass, Your word is my guide,
In the depths of my journey, I'll walk by Your side.
Through the highs and the lows, through joy and through strife,
As for me, I will serve the Lord; He's the source of my life."

Bible Verse:
"Your word is a lamp for my feet, a light on my path." (Psalm 119:105)

As for Me, I Will Serve the Lord

Inspirational Insight:
Context: Psalm 119:105 illustrates the guiding light of God's word. This verse reassures us that His teachings illuminate our journey. It connects with the poem by emphasizing the importance of His guidance.

Shining His Light
"Help me to shine Your light in a world that feels dark,
To share Your love freely, to ignite every spark.
In every action I take, may my heart be aligned,
As for me, I will serve the Lord; His purpose I find."

Bible Verse:
"Let your light shine before others, that they may see your good deeds and glorify your Father in heaven." (Matthew 5:16)

Inspirational Insight:
Context: Matthew 5:16 encourages us to be a light in the world. This verse reminds us that our actions reflect God's glory. It ties back to the poem by emphasizing our call to serve with purpose.

Questions for Personal Reflection or Group Discussion

- What does it mean to you to serve the Lord wholeheartedly?
- How can you remain steadfast in your commitment to serve amidst challenges?
- In what ways can you shine His light in your daily life?

My Walk With Him

Guided Prayer

- "Dear Lord, thank You for the opportunity to serve You. Help me to remain committed to Your calling and to trust in Your guidance. May my life reflect Your love and purpose, and may I always declare, as for me, I will serve the Lord. Amen."

Twenty-Five

To Whom Shall We Go

Hello again! In this chapter, we'll explore the theme of seeking refuge and guidance in God. Through heartfelt poetry, meaningful scripture, and uplifting insights, we'll reflect on the importance of turning to Him in times of uncertainty. Let's walk this path together and find hope and strength in our Savior.

To Whom Shall We Go

In the depths of my longing, when questions arise,
   I search for the answer beneath the vast skies.
   For when the world is confusing, and my heart feels low,
   To whom shall we go, Lord? Your truth is my glow.

When the storms start to gather, and fear grips my soul,
   Help me remember the promise that makes me whole.

For every doubt that I carry, every burden I tow,
    To whom shall we go, Lord? Your love I will know.

In the silence of struggle, when hope seems far away,
    Remind me, dear Savior, that You're with me each day.
    For every tear that I shed, every prayer that I sow,
    To whom shall we go, Lord? Your peace I will show.

Your words are my comfort, Your presence my song,
    In the journey of life, You help me be strong.
    Through the trials and triumphs, through joy and through woe,
    To whom shall we go, Lord? In You, I will grow.

Help me to share this truth with those who feel lost,
    To guide them to You, no matter the cost.
    In every moment I live, may my heart overflow,
    To whom shall we go, Lord? Your grace I will show.

Reflection

In this chapter, we explore the importance of seeking God as our ultimate source of guidance and comfort. From recognizing our need for Him to embracing His promises, we learn that turning to God transforms our struggles into strength. By relying on Him, we can navigate life's uncertainties.

This chapter encourages us to trust in His wisdom, find solace in His love, and share His truth with others. Let's continue this journey of faith, knowing that He is always the answer we seek.

To Whom Shall We Go

When We Look, What We Find

Seeking Answers
"In the depths of my longing, when questions arise,
I search for the answer beneath the vast skies.
For when the world is confusing, and my heart feels low,
To whom shall we go, Lord? Your truth is my glow."

Bible Verse:
"Lord, to whom shall we go? You have the words of eternal life." (John 6:68)

Inspirational Insight:
Context: John 6:68 highlights the disciples' recognition of Jesus as the source of eternal truth. This verse serves as a powerful reminder that our ultimate guidance comes from Him. It ties back to the poem by affirming our search for answers in Christ.

Facing Storms with Faith
"When the storms start to gather, and fear grips my soul,
Help me remember the promise that makes me whole.
For every doubt that I carry, every burden I tow,
To whom shall we go, Lord? Your love I will know."

Bible Verse:
"When you pass through the waters, I will be with you." (Isaiah 43:2)

Inspirational Insight:
Context: Isaiah 43:2 reassures us of God's presence in our

trials. This verse encourages us to rely on His protection and love. It connects with the poem by reminding us that we are never alone in our struggles.

Finding Hope in Silence

"In the silence of struggle, when hope seems far away,
Remind me, dear Savior, that You're with me each day.
For every tear that I shed, every prayer that I sow,
To whom shall we go, Lord? Your peace I will show."

Bible Verse:

"Cast all your anxiety on Him because He cares for you." (1 Peter 5:7)

Inspirational Insight:

Context: 1 Peter 5:7 emphasizes the importance of bringing our worries to God. This verse reassures us of His caring nature. It ties back to the poem by highlighting our need to seek His peace in times of distress.

Strength in His Presence

"Your words are my comfort, Your presence my song,
In the journey of life, You help me be strong.
Through the trials and triumphs, through joy and through woe,
To whom shall we go, Lord? In You, I will grow."

Bible Verse:

"The Lord is my strength and my shield; my heart trusts in Him, and He helps me." (Psalm 28:7)

To Whom Shall We Go

Inspirational Insight:

Context: Psalm 28:7 reassures us that God is our source of strength. This verse encourages us to trust in His help. It connects with the poem by emphasizing our growth through reliance on Him.

Sharing His Truth

"Help me to share this truth with those who feel lost,
To guide them to You, no matter the cost.
In every moment I live, may my heart overflow,
To whom shall we go, Lord? Your grace I will show."

Bible Verse:

"Go therefore and make disciples of all nations." (Matthew 28:19)

Inspirational Insight:

Context: Matthew 28:19 calls us to share the message of Christ with others. This verse reminds us of our mission to spread His love. It ties back to the poem by emphasizing our role in guiding others to Him.

Questions for Personal Reflection or Group Discussion

- In what areas of your life do you need to seek God's guidance?
- How can you remind yourself of His presence during difficult times?
- What steps can you take to share His truth with those around you?

My Walk With Him

Guided Prayer

- "Dear Lord, thank You for being my source of guidance and comfort. Help me to turn to You in times of uncertainty and to trust in Your promises. May my life reflect Your love, and may I lead others to You, for to whom shall we go but You? Amen."

Twenty-Six

Not My Will, But Your Will Be Done

Hello again! In this chapter, we'll explore the profound act of surrendering our desires to God's will. Through heartfelt poetry, meaningful scripture, and uplifting insights, we'll reflect on the beauty of yielding to His plans. Let's walk this path together and find hope and strength in our submission to Him.

Not My Will, But Yours Be Done

In the garden of my heart, where choices intertwine,
   I lay my dreams before You, Lord, trusting in Your design.
   Though my path may be unclear, and my plans may seem right,
   Not my will, but Yours be done; lead me into Your light.

When the world pulls me sideways, and doubts start to creep,

Help me remember the promise that Your love will keep.
For every fear that I face, every tear that I shed,
Not my will, but Yours be done; in Your arms, I am led.

In the silence of waiting, when answers feel far away,
Remind me, dear Savior, that You guide me each day.
For every prayer that I whisper, every sigh that I send,
Not my will, but Yours be done; Your grace is my friend.

Your purpose is my anchor, Your wisdom my guide,
In the journey of surrender, I'll trust in Your stride.
Through the highs and the lows, through joy and through pain,
Not my will, but Yours be done; in You, I remain.

Help me to embrace the path that You have laid out,
To follow where You lead me, to live without doubt.
In every moment I breathe, may my heart ever respond,
Not my will, but Yours be done; to You, I will bond.

Reflection

In this chapter, we explore the importance of surrendering our will to God. From recognizing our need for His guidance to embracing His plans, we learn that true peace comes from yielding to His purpose. By trusting in Him, we can navigate life's uncertainties with grace.

This chapter encourages us to find strength in submission, to seek His wisdom, and to live out our faith in every decision. Let's continue this journey of faith, knowing that His will is

Not My Will, But Your Will Be Done

always for our good.

When We Look, What We Find

Surrendering Our Dreams
"In the garden of my heart, where choices intertwine,
I lay my dreams before You, Lord, trusting in Your design.
Though my path may be unclear, and my plans may seem right,
Not my will, but Yours be done; lead me into Your light."

Bible Verse:
"Father, if You are willing, take this cup from me; yet not my will, but Yours be done." (Luke 22:42)

Inspirational Insight:
Context: Luke 22:42 captures Jesus' moment of surrender in Gethsemane. This verse serves as a powerful reminder of the importance of yielding to God's will. It ties back to the poem by affirming our need to trust His plan.

Facing Doubts with Faith
"When the world pulls me sideways, and doubts start to creep,
Help me remember the promise that Your love will keep.
For every fear that I face, every tear that I shed,
Not my will, but Yours be done; in Your arms, I am led."

Bible Verse:
"Cast all your anxiety on Him because He cares for you." (1 Peter 5:7)

Inspirational Insight:
Context: 1 Peter 5:7 emphasizes the importance of bringing our worries to God. This verse reassures us of His caring nature. It connects with the poem by highlighting our need to surrender our fears to Him.

Finding Peace in Waiting
"In the silence of waiting, when answers feel far away,
Remind me, dear Savior, that You guide me each day.
For every prayer that I whisper, every sigh that I send,
Not my will, but Yours be done; Your grace is my friend."

Bible Verse:
"Be still, and know that I am God." (Psalm 46:10)

Inspirational Insight:
Context: Psalm 46:10 calls us to find peace in God's presence. This verse encourages us to trust in His timing. It ties back to the poem by reminding us that waiting can be an opportunity for growth.

Anchored in His Purpose
"Your purpose is my anchor, Your wisdom my guide,
In the journey of surrender, I'll trust in Your stride.
Through the highs and the lows, through joy and through pain,
Not my will, but Yours be done; in You, I remain."

Bible Verse:
"For I know the plans I have for you, declares the Lord, plans to prosper you and not to harm you, plans to give you hope

Not My Will, But Your Will Be Done

and a future." (Jeremiah 29:11)

Inspirational Insight:
Context: Jeremiah 29:11 reassures us of God's good plans for our lives. This verse encourages us to trust in His purpose. It connects with the poem by emphasizing our reliance on His wisdom.

Walking in His Way
"Help me to embrace the path that You have laid out,
To follow where You lead me, to live without doubt.
In every moment I breathe, may my heart ever respond,
Not my will, but Yours be done; to You, I will bond."

Bible Verse:
"Trust in the Lord with all your heart and lean not on your own understanding." (Proverbs 3:5)

Inspirational Insight:
Context: Proverbs 3:5 encourages us to trust God over our own understanding. This verse reminds us of the importance of surrendering our will. It ties back to the poem by emphasizing the need for complete trust in Him.

Questions for Personal Reflection or Group Discussion

- What areas of your life do you find challenging to surrender to God?
- How can you remind yourself to trust in His timing and plans?

- In what ways can you encourage others to embrace God's will in their lives?

Guided Prayer

- "Dear Lord, thank You for the gift of surrender. Help me to lay down my will and trust in Your plans for my life. May I find peace in Your guidance, and may my heart always say, not my will, but Yours be done. Amen."

Twenty-Seven

He Is More Than Enough

Hello again! In this chapter, we'll explore the theme of God's sufficiency in our lives. Through heartfelt poetry, meaningful scripture, and uplifting insights, we'll reflect on how He meets our every need. Let's walk this path together and find hope and strength in His abundance.

He Is More Than Enough

In the depths of my longing, when I feel all alone,
  I turn to You, Lord, for You are my cornerstone.
  Though the world may leave me wanting, and my heart may feel tough,
  He is more than enough; Your love is my stuff.

When the trials surround me, and I'm weary and worn,
  Help me remember the promise that in You, I am reborn.

My Walk With Him

For every burden I carry, every fear that I face,
    He is more than enough; Your mercy is my grace.

In the moments of doubt, when my faith starts to shake,
    Remind me, dear Savior, that You'll never forsake.
    For every tear that I've cried, every prayer that I've prayed,
    He is more than enough; Your strength will not fade.

Your joy is my anchor, Your peace is my song,
    In the journey of life, You help me grow strong.
    Through the highs and the lows, through joy and through strife,
    He is more than enough; in You, I find life.

Help me to share this truth with those who feel lost,
    To point them to You, no matter the cost.
    In every moment I live, may my heart overflow,
    He is more than enough; Your love I will show.

Reflection

In this chapter, we explore the sufficiency of God in every aspect of our lives. From recognizing our needs to embracing His provision, we learn that in Him, we lack nothing. By trusting in His abundance, we can face life's challenges with confidence.

This chapter encourages us to find strength in His promises, to rely on His grace, and to share His love with others. Let's continue this journey of faith, knowing that He is always more than enough for us.

He Is More Than Enough

When We Look, What We Find

Finding Our Sufficiency
"In the depths of my longing, when I feel all alone,
I turn to You, Lord, for You are my cornerstone.
Though the world may leave me wanting, and my heart may feel tough,
He is more than enough; Your love is my stuff."

Bible Verse:
"And my God will meet all your needs according to the riches of His glory in Christ Jesus." (Philippians 4:19)

Inspirational Insight:
Context: Philippians 4:19 assures us that God will provide for our needs. This verse serves as a powerful reminder of His sufficiency. It ties back to the poem by affirming our trust in His provision.

Strength in Trials
"When the trials surround me, and I'm weary and worn,
Help me remember the promise that in You, I am reborn.
For every burden I carry, every fear that I face,
He is more than enough; Your mercy is my grace."

Bible Verse:
"My grace is sufficient for you, for my power is made perfect in weakness." (2 Corinthians 12:9)

Inspirational Insight:
Context: 2 Corinthians 12:9 emphasizes that God's grace is

sufficient in our weaknesses. This verse encourages us to rely on His strength. It connects with the poem by highlighting that His mercy sustains us.

Overcoming Doubt
"In the moments of doubt, when my faith starts to shake,
Remind me, dear Savior, that You'll never forsake.
For every tear that I've cried, every prayer that I've prayed,
He is more than enough; Your strength will not fade."

Bible Verse:
"When I am afraid, I put my trust in You." (Psalm 56:3)

Inspirational Insight:
Context: Psalm 56:3 reassures us that we can trust God in our fears. This verse reminds us of His constant presence. It ties back to the poem by emphasizing our reliance on Him during difficult times.

Joy and Peace in Him
"Your joy is my anchor, Your peace is my song,
In the journey of life, You help me grow strong.
Through the highs and the lows, through joy and through strife,
He is more than enough; in You, I find life."

Bible Verse:
"The joy of the Lord is your strength." (Nehemiah 8:10)

Inspirational Insight:
Context: Nehemiah 8:10 highlights the strength found in

He Is More Than Enough

God's joy. This verse encourages us to embrace His joy as our source of strength. It connects with the poem by affirming that our true life is found in Him.

Sharing His Abundance
"Help me to share this truth with those who feel lost,
To point them to You, no matter the cost.
In every moment I live, may my heart overflow,
He is more than enough; Your love I will show."

Bible Verse:
"Freely you have received; freely give." (Matthew 10:8)

Inspirational Insight:
Context: Matthew 10:8 calls us to share the gifts we've received from God. This verse reminds us of our mission to spread His love. It ties back to the poem by emphasizing our role in sharing His sufficiency with others.

Questions for Personal Reflection or Group Discussion

- In what areas of your life do you struggle to see God's sufficiency?
- How can you remind yourself of His provision during challenging times?
- In what ways can you share the truth of His abundance with others?

Guided Prayer

My Walk With Him

- "Dear Lord, thank You for being more than enough in my life. Help me to trust in Your provision and to find strength in Your grace. May I share Your love and sufficiency with those around me, reflecting Your goodness in all I do. Amen."

Twenty-Eight

You Are My Firm Foundation

Hello again! In this chapter, we'll explore the theme of God as our unwavering foundation. Through heartfelt poetry, meaningful scripture, and uplifting insights, we'll reflect on how He stabilizes our lives amid life's storms. Let's walk this path together and find hope and strength in His steadfastness.

You Are My Firm Foundation

In the shifting sands of life, where troubles often rise,
   I find my strength in You, Lord, beneath the endless skies.
   When the storms rage around me, and my heart feels the strain,
   You are my firm foundation; in You, I remain.

When the doubts start to whisper, and fear begins to creep,

My Walk With Him

    Help me remember Your promises, the ones that I keep.
    For every trial I face, every mountain I climb,
    You are my firm foundation; Your love is my rhyme.

In the chaos of the world, when my peace feels far away,
    Remind me, dear Savior, that You guide me each day.
    For every tear that I shed, every heartache I bear,
    You are my firm foundation; in You, I find care.

Your Word is my anchor, Your truth is my light,
    In the journey of faith, You lead me through the night.
    Through the highs and the lows, through joy and through pain,
    You are my firm foundation; in You, I sustain.

Help me to share this hope with those who feel lost,
    To point them to You, no matter the cost.
    In every moment I live, may my heart overflow,
    You are my firm foundation; Your love I will show.

Reflection

In this chapter, we explore the importance of having God as our foundation. From recognizing His stability to embracing His promises, we learn that He is our source of strength in every situation. By trusting in Him, we can navigate life's uncertainties with confidence.

This chapter encourages us to find security in His Word, to rely on His truth, and to share His steadfastness with others. Let's continue this journey of faith, knowing that He is our

You Are My Firm Foundation

firm foundation.

When We Look, What We Find

Finding Stability in Him
"In the shifting sands of life, where troubles often rise,
I find my strength in You, Lord, beneath the endless skies.
When the storms rage around me, and my heart feels the strain,
You are my firm foundation; in You, I remain."

Bible Verse:
"Therefore everyone who hears these words of mine and puts them into practice is like a wise man who built his house on the rock." (Matthew 7:24)

Inspirational Insight:
Context: Matthew 7:24 emphasizes the importance of building our lives on God's Word. This verse serves as a powerful reminder of His stability. It ties back to the poem by affirming our need to trust in Him as our rock.

Strength in Trials
"When the doubts start to whisper, and fear begins to creep,
Help me remember Your promises, the ones that I keep.
For every trial I face, every mountain I climb,
You are my firm foundation; Your love is my rhyme."

Bible Verse:
"Cast all your anxiety on Him because He cares for you." (1 Peter 5:7)

Inspirational Insight:

Context: 1 Peter 5:7 reassures us that we can bring our worries to God. This verse reminds us of His caring nature. It connects with the poem by highlighting our reliance on Him during difficult times.

Peace in Chaos
"In the chaos of the world, when my peace feels far away,
Remind me, dear Savior, that You guide me each day.
For every tear that I shed, every heartache I bear,
You are my firm foundation; in You, I find care."

Bible Verse:

"You will keep in perfect peace those whose minds are steadfast, because they trust in You." (Isaiah 26:3)

Inspirational Insight:

Context: Isaiah 26:3 emphasizes the peace found in trusting God. This verse encourages us to rely on His steadfastness. It ties back to the poem by affirming that true peace comes from Him.

Guided by His Truth
"Your Word is my anchor, Your truth is my light,
In the journey of faith, You lead me through the night.
Through the highs and the lows, through joy and through pain,
You are my firm foundation; in You, I sustain."

Bible Verse:

"Your word is a lamp for my feet, a light on my path." (Psalm

119:105)

Inspirational Insight:
Context: Psalm 119:105 highlights the guiding power of God's Word. This verse reassures us that His truth leads us. It connects with the poem by emphasizing our need for His light in our lives.

Sharing His Hope
"Help me to share this hope with those who feel lost,
To point them to You, no matter the cost.
In every moment I live, may my heart overflow,
You are my firm foundation; Your love I will show."

Bible Verse:
"Freely you have received; freely give." (Matthew 10:8)

Inspirational Insight:
Context: Matthew 10:8 calls us to share the gifts we've received from God. This verse reminds us of our mission to spread His love. It ties back to the poem by emphasizing our role in sharing His steadfastness with others.

Questions for Personal Reflection or Group Discussion

- In what areas of your life do you need to rely more on God as your foundation?
- How can you remind yourself of His promises during challenging times?
- In what ways can you encourage others to find their

stability in Him?

Guided Prayer

- "Dear Lord, thank You for being my firm foundation. Help me to trust in Your Word and rely on Your strength in every situation. May I share Your steadfast love with those around me, reflecting Your goodness in all I do. Amen."

Twenty-Nine

My Cross Cannot Compare

Hello again! In this chapter, we'll explore the theme of bearing our burdens in light of Christ's sacrifice. Through heartfelt poetry, meaningful scripture, and uplifting insights, we'll reflect on how our struggles pale in comparison to His love and grace. Let's walk this path together and find hope and strength in His redemptive work.

My Cross Cannot Compare

In the shadows of my trials, when the weight feels too great,
   I lift my eyes to Jesus, who carried my fate.
      Though my burdens are heavy, and my heart feels the strain,
   My cross cannot compare to the love He did gain.

When the road becomes weary, and my spirit feels low,
   Help me remember the promise that in Him, I can grow.

For every tear that I've shed, every heartache I've known,
My cross cannot compare to the grace He has shown.

In the moments of doubt, when my faith starts to wane,
Remind me, dear Savior, of the joy in the pain.
For every trial I endure, every valley I face,
My cross cannot compare to the depth of His grace.

Your sacrifice is my anchor, Your love is my song,
In the journey of faith, You help me grow strong.
Through the highs and the lows, through joy and through strife,
My cross cannot compare to the gift of new life.

Help me to share this truth with those who feel lost,
To point them to You, no matter the cost.
In every moment I live, may my heart overflow,
My cross cannot compare to the love I will show.

Reflection

In this chapter, we explore the significance of our struggles in light of Christ's ultimate sacrifice. From recognizing the weight of our burdens to embracing His grace, we learn that our challenges are small compared to His love. By trusting in Him, we can endure life's trials with hope.

This chapter encourages us to find strength in His sacrifice, to rely on His grace, and to share His love with others. Let's continue this journey of faith, knowing that our crosses cannot compare to His.

My Cross Cannot Compare

When We Look, What We Find

Bearing Our Burdens
"In the shadows of my trials, when the weight feels too great,
I lift my eyes to Jesus, who carried my fate.
Though my burdens are heavy, and my heart feels the strain,
My cross cannot compare to the love He did gain."

Bible Verse:
"Come to me, all you who are weary and burdened, and I will give you rest." (Matthew 11:28)

Inspirational Insight:
Context: Matthew 11:28 invites us to bring our burdens to Christ. This verse serves as a comforting reminder of His willingness to carry our weight. It ties back to the poem by affirming our need for His rest.

Strength in Struggles
"When the road becomes weary, and my spirit feels low,
Help me remember the promise that in Him, I can grow.
For every tear that I've shed, every heartache I've known,
My cross cannot compare to the grace He has shown."

Bible Verse:
"He will wipe every tear from their eyes." (Revelation 21:4)

Inspirational Insight:
Context: Revelation 21:4 assures us of God's promise to comfort us. This verse reminds us that our pain is temporary. It connects with the poem by highlighting the hope we have in

My Walk With Him

His grace.

Joy in Pain
"In the moments of doubt, when my faith starts to wane,
Remind me, dear Savior, of the joy in the pain.
For every trial I endure, every valley I face,
My cross cannot compare to the depth of His grace."

Bible Verse:
"Consider it pure joy, my brothers and sisters, whenever you face trials of many kinds." (James 1:2)

Inspirational Insight:
Context: James 1:2 encourages us to see trials as opportunities for growth. This verse challenges us to find joy in our struggles. It ties back to the poem by emphasizing the purpose behind our pain.

Anchored in His Love
"Your sacrifice is my anchor, Your love is my song,
In the journey of faith, You help me grow strong.
Through the highs and the lows, through joy and through strife,
My cross cannot compare to the gift of new life."

Bible Verse:
"For God so loved the world that He gave His one and only Son." (John 3:16)

Inspirational Insight:
Context: John 3:16 highlights the depth of God's love

through Christ's sacrifice. This verse reassures us of the new life we have in Him. It connects with the poem by affirming the gift we receive through His love.

Sharing His Love
"Help me to share this truth with those who feel lost,
To point them to You, no matter the cost.
In every moment I live, may my heart overflow,
My cross cannot compare to the love I will show."

Bible Verse:
"Freely you have received; freely give." (Matthew 10:8)

Inspirational Insight:
Context: Matthew 10:8 calls us to share the gifts we've received from God. This verse reminds us of our mission to spread His love. It ties back to the poem by emphasizing our role in sharing His grace with others.

Questions for Personal Reflection or Group Discussion

- How do you perceive your struggles in light of Christ's sacrifice?
- In what ways can you find joy amid your trials?
- How can you encourage others to see the grace in their struggles?

Guided Prayer

My Walk With Him

- "Dear Lord, thank You for bearing my burdens and for the incredible gift of Your grace. Help me to trust in You during my trials and to share Your love with those around me. May my heart overflow with gratitude for the sacrifice You made for me. Amen."

Thirty

Lead Me Home

Hello again! In this chapter, we'll explore the theme of finding our true home in Christ. Through heartfelt poetry, meaningful scripture, and uplifting insights, we'll reflect on the journey of faith that leads us to Him. Let's walk this path together and find hope and strength in His guidance.

Lead Me Home

In the wanderings of my heart, when I feel far away,
   I lift my voice to You, Lord, to guide me each day.
     Though the road may be winding, and the path may feel long,
   Lead me home to Your presence; in You, I belong.

When the trials surround me, and my spirit feels worn,
   Help me remember the promise that in You, I'm reborn.
   For every step that I take, every choice that I make,

My Walk With Him

Lead me home to Your love; my heart You will wake.

In the moments of doubt, when I can't see the way,
   Remind me, dear Savior, that You're with me each day.
   For every tear that I've cried, every prayer that I've prayed,
   Lead me home to Your peace; in You, I am stayed.

Your Word is my compass, Your truth is my guide,
   In the journey of faith, You walk by my side.
   Through the highs and the lows, through joy and through strife,
   Lead me home to Your heart; in You, I find life.

Help me to share this journey with those who feel lost,
   To point them to You, no matter the cost.
   In every moment I live, may my heart overflow,
   Lead me home to Your love; Your grace I will show.

Reflection

In this chapter, we explore the journey of faith that brings us closer to God. From recognizing our longing for home to embracing His guidance, we learn that He is always leading us toward His love. By trusting in Him, we can navigate life's challenges with hope.

This chapter encourages us to find direction in His Word, to rely on His presence, and to share His love with others. Let's continue this journey of faith, knowing that He is leading us home.

Lead Me Home

When We Look, What We Find

Finding Our True Home
"In the wanderings of my heart, when I feel far away,
I lift my voice to You, Lord, to guide me each day.
Though the road may be winding, and the path may feel long,
Lead me home to Your presence; in You, I belong."

Bible Verse:
"For I know the plans I have for you, declares the Lord, plans to prosper you and not to harm you, plans to give you hope and a future." (Jeremiah 29:11)

Inspirational Insight:
Context: Jeremiah 29:11 reassures us of God's good plans for our lives. This verse serves as a comforting reminder that He is guiding us toward our true home. It ties back to the poem by affirming our trust in His direction.

Strength in Trials
"When the trials surround me, and my spirit feels worn,
Help me remember the promise that in You, I'm reborn.
For every step that I take, every choice that I make,
Lead me home to Your love; my heart You will wake."

Bible Verse:
"Cast all your anxiety on Him because He cares for you." (1 Peter 5:7)

Inspirational Insight:
Context: 1 Peter 5:7 invites us to bring our worries to God.

This verse reminds us of His caring nature. It connects with the poem by highlighting our need to rely on His love during difficult times.

Guidance in Doubt
"In the moments of doubt, when I can't see the way,
Remind me, dear Savior, that You're with me each day.
For every tear that I've cried, every prayer that I've prayed,
Lead me home to Your peace; in You, I am stayed."

Bible Verse:
"The Lord will guide you always; He will satisfy your needs in a sun-scorched land." (Isaiah 58:11)

Inspirational Insight:
Context: Isaiah 58:11 emphasizes God's promise to guide and provide for us. This verse reassures us that He is with us on our journey. It ties back to the poem by affirming His presence in our lives.

Anchored in His Word
"Your Word is my compass, Your truth is my guide,
In the journey of faith, You walk by my side.
Through the highs and the lows, through joy and through strife,
Lead me home to Your heart; in You, I find life."

Bible Verse:
"Your word is a lamp for my feet, a light on my path." (Psalm 119:105)

Lead Me Home

Inspirational Insight:

Context: Psalm 119:105 highlights the guiding power of God's Word. This verse reassures us that His truth illuminates our path. It connects with the poem by emphasizing our need for His light in our lives.

Sharing His Love

"Help me to share this journey with those who feel lost,
To point them to You, no matter the cost.
In every moment I live, may my heart overflow,
Lead me home to Your love; Your grace I will show."

Bible Verse:

"Freely you have received; freely give." (Matthew 10:8)

Inspirational Insight:

Context: Matthew 10:8 calls us to share the gifts we've received from God. This verse reminds us of our mission to spread His love. It ties back to the poem by emphasizing our role in guiding others toward His grace.

Questions for Personal Reflection or Group Discussion

- In what ways do you feel distant from God, and how can you seek His presence?
- How can you find peace in His guidance during uncertain times?
- How can you encourage others to join you on the journey home to Christ?

My Walk With Him

Guided Prayer

- "Dear Lord, thank You for leading me on this journey of faith. Help me to trust in Your guidance and to share Your love with those around me. May my heart always seek to be closer to You, knowing that You are my true home. Amen."

Afterword

Dear Reader,

As we come to the close of this book, I want to take a moment to express my heartfelt gratitude to you for embarking on this journey of faith and discovery with me. Your willingness to explore these pages, to reflect on the poems, scriptures, and insights shared, has made this experience truly meaningful.

When I first set out to write this book, I had no idea of the profound impact it would have on me. Each chapter has been a step in our shared pilgrimage, a chance to delve deeper into the wellsprings of faith and find renewed strength in God's presence.

Through the valleys of doubt and the mountaintops of joy, through moments of weariness and times of triumph, we've walked together. We've explored the depths of God's love, the power of His grace, and the comfort of His presence. My hope is that these words have been a source of encouragement, a reminder of God's faithfulness, and a catalyst for your own

My Walk With Him

spiritual growth.

Remember, this journey doesn't end with the closing of this book. The insights we've gained, the truths we've explored, and the prayers we've shared are meant to be lived out day by day. May you continue to find strength in your weariness, hope in your struggles, and joy in your walk with God.

Thank you for your open heart, your thoughtful reflections, and your companionship on this path. Your presence on this journey has been a blessing, and I'm grateful for the opportunity to share these moments with you.

As you move forward from here, may you always remember that you are loved, you are valued, and you are never alone. God's strength is with you, empowering you to prevail through every challenge and celebrate every victory.

With deepest appreciation and blessings for your continued journey,

Charlie

Made in United States
Orlando, FL
29 October 2024